Shrines
of
Our Lady
in England

*For John, without whom this book
could not have been written*

Shrines
of
Our Lady
in England

Anne Vail

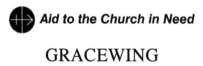

Aid to the Church in Need

GRACEWING

First published in 2004
Reprinted 2008

Gracewing
2 Southern Avenue
Leominster
Herefordshire HR6 0QF

The map of shrines of Our Lady by Tim Madden, is reproduced by
kind permission of Ladyewell shrine

ISBN 978 0 85244 603 4

Special edition printed in 2008 by arrangement with
Gracewing Publishing for:
⊕ Aid to the Church in Need
12–14 Benhill Avenue, Sutton, Surry, SM1 4DA
Registered with the Charity Commission No. 1097984

Typesetting by
Action Publishing Technology Ltd, Gloucester, GL1 5SR

Printed in England by
Athenaeum Press Ltd, Gateshead NE11 0PZ

Contents

Acknowledgements

I would like to express my gratitude to those who have so kindly given of their time and knowledge in the preparation of this book and particularly to Ann Hutley whose initial suggestion it was that set me on my journey. On many occasions the unsung heroes of the shrines of Our Lady are the incumbent priests whose knowledge and enthusiasm they share so generously.

I am indebted to Father Wilfrid McGreal, O Carm of the Friars at Aylesford, Abbot David Charlesworth, OSB of Buckfast Abbey, and at Caversham, Father Anthony Jones. Father David Middleton, OSA of Clare in Suffolk, and at Coventry, Monsignor Patrick Kilgarriff. Father Augustus O'Reilly of Doncaster and at Glastonbury, Abbot Charles Fitzgerald Lombard. At Hartley, Father Hugh Bridge, at King's Lynn, Father David Finegan and Father Benedict Ruscillo of Ladyewell in Lancashire. At Osmotherley Father Terence Richardson, OSB, the Hon. Piers Grant-Ferris, OSB and Father Anthony Storey. Father Damian Sturdy, OSB of Prinknash Abbey, and Father Peter Rollings of Sudbury. Father Malachy Sheehan, OMI at Tower Hill, and at Warwick Street, Monsignor James Overton and Canon R.G. Fuller. Father David Goddard at West Grinstead and Father Nicholas Schofield at Willesden.

I would like to thank Sister Elizabeth Obbard, CS who explained the spirit of Carmel and made the point that pilgrimage was and is for everyone – a great leveller. The Dominican Sisters of Stone in Staffordshire were so welcoming and I particularly wish to thank Sister Mary Henry, OP and Sister Mary Alberta, OP. The Revd Michael Fisher described aspects of the Pugin chapel at Stone and I learnt much from his excellent book *Pugin Land*. Morag, Lady Stafford was a mine of information about the role of the Staffords at the time of the Reformation and in later centuries and was generous with her time.

I would like to thank Sister Stephanie Dalton, Sister of Providence, of the shrine of Our Lady of Doncaster, Antonia Moffat at Walsingham, Catherine Woolmer at Glastonbury, Charles Weld of Chideock and Prue Porretta at Coventry.

Dr Maire Heley was unstintingly generous with her time and great knowledge of the Shrine of Our Lady of Grace of Ipswich and I am very grateful to her.

A considerable debt is due to Mrs Maureen Jupp, the Warden of Westminster Abbey who gave generously of her valuable time and expertise in describing the Shrine of Our Lady of Pew. I would also like to thank Mr Gordon Amand for explaining the contribution of his relation, Mr Albert Freeman, in donating the magnificent statue at Pew, and also for the description written by Sister Concordia Scott of the discovery of the stone that was used in the carving. I am grateful to Sister Concordia for her permission to quote from that source and I would like to thank her for the time I spent with her.

I am most grateful to Mrs Audrey Peniston for sharing her knowledge of the shrine of Our Lady and St Pirin in Truro.

I would like to thank Helen Coker for the directions to each of these shrines and, although every effort has been made to ensure accuracy, alterations are unavoidable and it would be wise to check the information before setting out.

I wish to thank Sarah Boss of The Centre for Marian Studies at the University of Wales in Lampeter whose original notes she kindly allowed me to use.

I could not have had more encouraging publishers than Tom Longford and Jo Ashworth of Gracewing. My debt is great to Teresa de Bertodano who has woven coherence from confusion and who has brilliantly averted unwitting mistakes – the book has gained immeasurably from her editing expertise and I am so grateful to her.

This book could not have been completed without the help and support of so many people. The remaining shortcomings are my own. Every effort has been made to verify facts. I ask the indulgence of those concerned and that they will get in touch with me so that appropriate adjustment and acknowledgement may be made in future editions.

I am most grateful to His Eminence, Cardinal Cormac Murphy-O'Connor for writing the Foreword.

Foreword

It gives me great pleasure to write a few words of appreciation for this book on the Shrines of Our Lady by Anne Vail. It is, indeed, a labour of love. The author herself has visited and prayed at many of these shrines of our Blessed Lady about which she writes. The idea of 'pilgrimage' is a very rich and important one in the history of the Church and I sincerely hope that Anne Vail's book will not only encourage a greater devotion to Our Lady but also be an encouragement to visit one or other of the English Shrines that are mentioned in the book. I warmly commend it and hope it is widely read.

+Cormac Cardinal Murphy. O'Connor

+Cormac Card. Murphy-O'Connor
Archbishop of Westminster

Map showing shrines of Our Lady in England. Twenty-eight shrines are described in the book. (The shrines at Clare, Hartley and Truro are not shown on this map.)

Introduction

There are more than sixty shrines in honour of Our Lady in England. Unlike Lourdes, Fatima and other world-famous sanctuaries, the English shrines are not always places where apparitions have occurred and they are, for the most part, small and unpublicized. With few exceptions, they were founded in the thirteenth and fourteenth centuries and were recognized as places of pilgrimage. A shrine was named in honour of the Blessed Virgin and after the place in which it stood – Our Lady of Walsingham, for example, or Our Lady of Lincoln. Sometimes a particular characteristic had a bearing on the name: Our Lady of Consolation at West Grinstead, or Our Lady of Good Counsel at Clare.

At the turn of the millennium I went on a pilgrimage. From all corners of England small groups of people were on the move to visit the web of shrines of Our Lady that was once part of the geography of this country. We were to rediscover lost shrines, to visit others which were known to exist although hidden and frequently maintained by devoted custodians, and to join the crowds at the more famous landmarks on the pilgrim route.

Within a year, our plan that had seemed ambitious at the time was completed, and this book is one result of our pilgrimage, as I returned to explore some of the extraordinary places that we visited.

In city centre or small village, in the depths of the country or on the bleak northern moors, these shrines had been places of prayer for centuries, and the paths worn by the pilgrims' steps across the land trace the skeleton of Our Lady's Dowry in England.

There is frequently some difficulty in discovering precisely why the site of a shrine was chosen. Sometimes there was a dream or a vision, as in the case of Evesham. There were often rumours of miracles, for the people of the Middle Ages were not sceptical and they expected such things to happen. The saints were their friends and they turned to them in prayer in all the vicissitudes of their lives. These places were founded in thanksgiving for prayers answered, in honour of the saints, and above all in honour of Our Lady. Kings and commoners turned aside from their daily routine and made their way to Our Lady of Glastonbury, to Our Lady of Caversham and the many other shrines.

In England the shrines sometimes have particular links with the sea. Our Lady of Grace at Tower Hill was founded by a grateful King Edward III who had been saved from shipwreck. Fergus Maguire of Fernyhalgh wandered the Lancashire lanes for days in an attempt to find the spot in which he had been told to build a chapel in thanksgiving for deliverance from shipwreck. On many such occasions the shrine was handed over to a religious foundation for the day-to-day running: in the case of Our Lady of Grace the King gave the shrine to the Carmelites.

In Worcestershire, Eoves the swineherd saw a vision of a beautiful maiden with two attendants. He hurried away to tell the bishop who came to see for himself. It was indeed the Virgin, and Eoves is commemorated in the name of the town of Evesham in which a great shrine was built. The origin of the shrine of Our Lady of Willesden is perhaps less certain, although it was believed that Our Lady had been seen in an oak tree in the churchyard. Most famous of all is perhaps the dream of Richeldis which resulted in the great shrine of Our Lady of Walsingham.

No less important were the powerful families in their encouragement of devotion to the Blessed Virgin. In the west country, the Arundells of Lanherne were a strong influence. In Suffolk the de Clares had an impact that spread far beyond their own county, and the Giffards are lovingly remembered at Prinknash and further afield. Most important of all was perhaps the Lady Godgifu of Coventry, often known as Godiva, and her husband Leofric, Earl of Mercia. These men and women used their wealth and power in the service of their deep Christian faith.

In medieval England, despite the accoutrements of royalty that might separate a king from his people, life could be described as 'nasty, brutish and short' for rich and poor alike. King, noble and commoner, all were aware that they entered and departed the world in the same manner. There was a bond among those who travelled the lanes, for these shrines were for the people, no matter who they might be. All were united in their anxieties and in their trust in the advocacy of their saints.

In a world that was satirized so graphically by Chaucer, pilgrimage was a way of life. As soon as spring came gently to replace the icy winter winds, the pilgrim felt a longing to be on his way, in the company of friends, with gossip and stories to be shared and songs to be sung. In May, the month of Mary, briar roses were gathered from the hedges, as pilgrims made their way south to Canterbury or westwards to Glastonbury.

Shrines were filled with images of Mary or of the beloved saint, just as we surround ourselves with pictures of those we love: to suggest that it is the picture which we love is ridiculous; rather, it brings to the mind's eye the one we long to see.

Gifts were brought to the shrine and laid at the feet of the statue as a token of affection, but also with the desire to 'remind' Our Lady or the special saint of the donor's existence, so that even when the pilgrim departed, the memory of his presence might linger.

The lists of these gifts make revealing reading. To reformers they were proof of outrageous extravagance, and in the scramble for scapegoats and plunder the true motives behind such gestures were frequently overlooked and misunderstood. Until the Dissolution of the monasteries there was no financial gain to be acquired from precious objects left at a shrine. However, the crowds swelled as the fame spread of the magnificence of one shrine over another, and in that sense gifts were indeed a diversion from the prayer of pilgrimage.

By far the greatest number of shrines in England were dedicated to Our Lady. The immediacy with which Mary was viewed in the Middle Ages is brought home by the figures made in her image at the time. Many of the statues show a young smiling mother holding her child who smiles in return. She is strong and she dresses simply, a woman who understands the hardships of life and looks with love and compassion on those who seek her.

England was her acknowledged dowry, and the people turned with trust to this 'sweet maiden' whose faith in the word of God strengthened their own. They believed that she understood their plight and would show them the way to her Son. It was a bond that seemed indestructible, so deeply was it implanted in the English mind.

Some of the gifts brought to shrines illustrate the intimate affection in which Mary was held. No sooner was the birth of his short-lived son, Prince Henry, announced in 1511 than Henry VIII hurried to East Barsham Manor outside Walsingham. Removing his shoes, the King walked barefoot to the shrine to place a necklace on the statue of Our Lady in thanksgiving. Years later, as Henry lay dying, he was overheard bequeathing his soul into the care of Our Lady of Walsingham.

During the Hundred Years War (1337–1443), the Earl of Sussex left a silver statuette of himself, fully armed and mounted on his horse, to remind Our Lady of Walsingham that he was off to fight the French.

According to legend, King Arthur carried the image of Mary painted on the inside of his shield so that he could see her when going into battle. Arthur apparently returned to Glastonbury to be buried under the protection of Our Lady.

Women too came with gifts for Mary, often leaving girdles inscribed with the Magnificat, which were worn during pregnancy in the hope of a safe delivery. In 1449, Constance Bigod left her girdle worked with silver gilt to Our Lady of Doncaster. Alice West left a simple bequest: 'To Our Lady of Doncaster; my best bedes'.

It would be hard to imagine such highly personal gifts being showered upon the woman illustrated by artists of later generations. After the sixteenth century, the portrayal of Our Lady altered almost beyond recognition. Artists depicted a remote and solemn figure swathed in velvets and silks, frequently looking towards skies which were filled with rotund cherubs defying the laws of gravity. Such a being was far removed from the figure who walked the roads of the Holy Land and followed the steps of her Son to Calvary.

In the sixteenth century, the great abbeys and centres of pilgrimage disappeared and a pall of silence fell on a land that had once echoed with laughter as well as prayer. It is impossible to tell the stories of the shrines without recounting those dark days.

How easy to point to Henry VIII and his chief minister, Thomas Cromwell, as the villains of the piece. Some historians emphasize the challenges of Martin Luther, others draw attention to the failures of the Church itself. There was spiritual anarchy in many parts of Europe, and grave wrongs were committed which led to war and revolution. The echoes reverberate to this day.

In England, Cardinal Wolsey was placed in charge of the King's Great Matter, the attempt to obtain from the Pope an annulment of Henry's marriage to Catherine of Aragon. Wolsey failed to produce the desired result, and fell from grace. In 1532 Henry extracted from the convocation of Canterbury an agreement which surrendered to the Crown the freedom to legislate about the English Church. This precipitated the resignation of Thomas More, Wolsey's successor as chancellor. In 1534 the Supremacy of the Crown Act confirmed to Henry and his successors the title of 'the only supreme head in earth of the Church in England'.

Gradually changes were wrought in public worship, and anything that remained of the ways of Rome was obliterated. The few men and women who stood out against the desecration that followed met with torture and death. The majority of the population either retreated into silence or accepted the inevitable.

By 1536 most of the small monasteries had gone, and by 1539 larger ones had suffered the same fate. The last monasteries surrendered in the spring of 1540.

For three hundred years, the shrines of the Blessed Virgin in England remained untenanted. Meanwhile the courage and sacrifice of recusant families enabled countless 'ordinary' Catholics to persevere in their faith.

After the 1829 Act of Catholic Emancipation, shrines began to reopen. At first Catholics were circumspect and somewhat inhibited, and they were slow to return to the shrines in any number. In 1897, an official announcement from the Pope restored the shrine of Our Lady of Walsingham at King's Lynn, prior to its eventual re-establishment at Walsingham itself. In the words of Pope Leo XIII, 'When England returns to Walsingham, Our Lady will return to England'. The lanes of Suffolk and Norfolk are filled once more with pilgrims who wend their way to Walsingham, and many also visit the East Anglian shrines of Clare, Sudbury and Ipswich, and the ruins of Thetford Priory.

Although thousands of pilgrims visit Walsingham every year, the scars of separation are still in evidence. In the 1920s Father Alfred Hope Patten created a magnificent Anglo-Catholic shrine at Walsingham and prayed deeply for the healing of wounds between Christians. He ensured that stones from the monasteries dismantled during the Reformation should be included in the walls of the new building. The main altar includes stone from the original altar of Walsingham Priory.

In 1981 Cardinal Hume opened the new Catholic chapel in honour of 'Our Lady of Reconciliation' at Walsingham and expressed his hope that prayers would be offered there for the unity of all Christians. Until that time, the reality of Our Lady's Dowry remains an unfulfilled dream.

There is a belief that the dream of Christian unity may be achieved through the shrines of Mary. They are simple places of prayer, far from hierarchy, precedent and the burden of decision. On the back of the statue of Our Lady of Pew in Westminster Abbey are the words, 'That they may all be one'.

The work of distinguished artists is filling the niches left empty for so many years; in the hands of the Benedictine sculptor, Sister Concordia Scott, the image of Mary is returning to the figure beloved of the medieval church. These figures reveal a woman of steadfast courage and peace, no longer laughing, but with the ghost of a smile as she presents her Son to the world in loving concern for the men and women of today. Occasionally she wears a fine Saxon crown, as at Coventry and Canterbury.

Pilgrimage is once again part of the Christian way of life, for few would deny the longing to escape the demands of the moment, to cast aside all that blurs our vision of those things that we recognize to matter above all others. In walking the pilgrim way there is an awakening sense of proportion as we are brought face to face with the loving concern of heaven in all that we do and all that we are.

As we neared the end of our pilgrimage, the words of an earlier pilgrim came frequently to mind: they could describe any one of Our Lady's shrines. 'The walls seem to be impregnated with prayer: there appears to be a whisper of prayer breathing around the place and the walls seem to give out and to surround you with an atmosphere of prayer ... The very stones appear to have been mesmerised by the power of prayer, great the peace to be obtained here by prayer.' (*The Month*, vol. iv, p. 40).

AYLESFORD

1

Aylesford

The first impression of Aylesford Priory, known as 'The Friars', is not one of monastic stillness. We are close to the Kent town of Maidstone, and to the east of the priory lies the belching mass of Aylesford Newsprint, and to the north the ceaseless drum of the M20 motorway. But once immersed in the shrine, these oppressive neighbours are forgotten: the atmosphere is one of peace and at the same time there is no mistaking the efficient organization that makes up this celebrated priory.

In a summer of torpid heat, I arrive at Aylesford Priory in the early morning as the mist rises and lingers over the lawns. Silence envelops chapels and cloisters, courtyards and workshops; the river, green in the mid-summer heat, meanders slowly past and an occasional moorhen darts into the shadows.

Immaculately-groomed lawns and wide sweeping paths lead beside clipped hedges and past the lake to a black swan preening elegantly on the grass in the centre of the ancient courtyard. Standing beside the River Medway, this group of buildings, with its medieval cells and magnificent Pilgrims' Hall, now used as the dining hall, forms part of the gift of a thirteenth-century crusader to the Carmelite friars. It contains one of the oldest medieval courtyards in England to remain intact, and is now once more the home of the Carmelite order.

The Carmelite friars take their name from Mount Carmel in the Holy Land, the dwelling-place of the prophet Elijah whom the early friars of the twelfth century took as the model for their contemplative life on Mount Carmel. Each Carmelite hermit was alloted a cave dwelling where he was to remain day and night praying continually, and the order was placed under the particular protection of the Blessed Virgin. By the middle of the thirteenth century, the peaceful tenor of their hermit existence was becoming increasingly threatened by the instability of their crusader kingdom, and friars began to migrate to Europe.

At Aylesford the turmoil of the years of the Crusades is graphically portrayed on the walls of the Pilgrims' Hall in a series of modern paintings by the Polish artist Adam Kossowski. The Saracens appear mounted on warhorses, their ferocious demeanour only slightly mitigated by the splendour of their apparel, for they have clad themselves in all their finery to intimidate the simple friars of Mount Carmel. But the friars turn in prayer to their patroness, the Blessed Virgin, and their prayers are heard.

In 1242 a group make their way to England at the invitation of the crusader knight, Richard de Grey, who has offered them a home at Aylesford. Subsequent pictures show the friars reading and praying in their new cells in holy contentment.

By 1248 work is under way on a church in honour of the Assumption of the Glorious Virgin, and Kossowski's pictures show the friars bricklaying and stonecutting. In the distance we see the bridge across the River Medway which pilgrims will cross on their journey to the priory. The Friars was on the ancient pilgrim route to the shrines of St Thomas Becket and of Our Lady Undercroft at Canterbury Cathedral, and there would have been a constant stream of pilgrims wishing to rest here before the final leg of their journey to Canterbury.

The next picture tells the story of the dissolution of Aylesford Priory in 1538. The formidable figure of King Henry VIII's chief minister, Thomas Cromwell, reads an order of expulsion as the friars turn to leave their beloved home. Above the bridge across the Medway stands the figure of Mary, her mantle held wide to protect the sad procession of friars going into exile.

In the final picture, Our Lady stands above the Aylesford gatehouse, the edges of her cloak held by angels, as the friars return to their home in 1949 after an absence of nearly four hundred years. This is the gateway through which the friars departed in 1538, and above the opening there is a statue of Our Lady restored to its place to greet whoever enters The Friars.

For twenty years the artist Adam Kossowski worked on pictures and ceramics for the restored buildings at Aylesford, in thanksgiving for his release from imprisonment. Kossowski had been captured in Warsaw in 1939, and was held for three years of the Second World War in a slave labour camp in the Soviet Union. The work he has bequeathed to Aylesford expresses the joy of one whose hope remained undiminished by the experience of suffering and exile.

There are nearly a hundred examples of Kossowski's work here. Each of the restored chapels is enriched by his vision of the world: of the evil of those who tormented Jesus; of the supercilious glances of the scribes in the temple; and of the purity and holiness of Mary and Joseph, whose faces are almost iconic in their beauty. At the top of many of the paintings, angels fly urgently through star-filled skies to bring the words of heaven to an anxious people on earth. These radiant works are indeed an invitation to prayer and meditation.

I leave the Pilgrims' Hall and pass through a cool stone passageway into the cloister chapel of St Jude and the Infant Jesus of Prague. Banks of candles glow in the darkness, and the luminous colours of the Flower of Carmel window, 'Flos Carmeli', dispel the shadows that surround the statue of St Jude the Apostle.

Beside a small series of the Stations of the Cross by Kossowski there hangs a stone plaque with the words: 'Alice Woolsey Hewitt 1876–1947, who loved this place, restored the chapel and rebuilt what fire had destroyed.' In 1920 Alice and her husband Copley Hewitt bought The Friars, which had previously been rented from the Earls of Aylesford by her mother-in-law. The work they undertook to restore the buildings was severely hampered by a fire that swept through the buildings in 1930. Although much of the property was destroyed, no one was harmed, and the transformation of The Friars to medieval splendour was rapidly resumed. Alice Hewitt died in 1947; her husband then started negotiating a Carmelite return to Aylesford, and in 1949 Father Malachy Lynch became the first prior after the restoration. He and his religious brothers built on the work of Alice and Copley Hewitt and set about the renovation of the buildings with unflagging energy, to serve the needs of the thousands of pilgrims who make their way here each year.

Beyond the cloister chapel of St Jude and the Infant of Prague is a chapel dedicated to St Anne, the mother of Our Lady. Here the story of St Anne and her husband Joachim is told in a rhythmic series of ceramics that seem to dance across the walls, culminating in the image of St Anne leading her daughter Mary into the temple beneath the dignified gaze of the high priest. The image of the devoted grandparents of Jesus with their small daughter Mary is timeless, ordinary and sublime at the same time, and one to which all can respond at the deepest level, an unmistakable awareness of the intimacy of family life which lies at the heart of Christianity.

On many days of the year, vast crowds gather at The Friars for organized pilgrimages, and outside in the piazza there is open-air seating in front of the shrine statue of the Glorious Virgin of the Assumption standing against the background of a star-strewn sky. But Aylesford is also a place for individuals and for family groups.

On the day of my visit I noticed a man tenderly carrying his small child up the steps to the statue of Our Lady where they both knelt, the rest of the family standing quietly beside them. Some time later, I caught sight of them eating their picnic by the lake with an air of peaceful contentment, and watching a Muscovy duck with her ducklings.

The main shrine is surrounded by smaller chapels, designed by Adrian Gilbert Scott, son of the distinguished architect, Sir Giles Gilbert Scott, and inspired by the prior, Father Malachy.

Carmel is known as the order of Our Lady, and in the statue in the piazza we see a tall figure dressed in the simplest of garments, her steadfast gaze fixed on heaven, and the shadow of a smile softening her glance. Her beauty is that of a young woman who has lived and worked like other people; a woman whose feet are strong from walking the stony paths of Galilee. She is the fruitful vine we read of in the Psalms, the woman who is inseparable from her Son: the silent but by no means impassive observer of all that took place on the road to Calvary, where she remained to the end. The only sign of gentleness in the figure in the Aylesford piazza appears in the slender hands open towards heaven. The twelfth-century Carmelite friars chose to be known as the 'Order of the Brothers of Our Lady of Mount Carmel', for their lives were spent in meditation on the Scriptures, following the example of the Blessed Virgin who 'pondered these things in her heart' (Luke 2.19, 51) This carved Madonna conveys everything that drew the early hermits to seek her protection.

The Scapular

The story of the Scapular Apparition is an important part of Carmelite tradition. According to legend, Our Lady appeared to the thirteenth-century prior general of the Carmelites, St Simon Stock, who was an Englishman. Simon held out to her his scapular (the piece of cloth worn over the shoulders and hanging down across the front and back of the garment beneath), Our Lady touched the scapular, and graciously promised her protection to all who wear this garment, which has always formed part of the Carmelite habit. In the reliquary chapel at Aylesford a magnificent black and gold structure holds the skull of St Simon, who died in 1265. The relic had been held in Bordeaux since the death of the

saint, and was transferred to Aylesford by the Archbishop of
Bordeaux in 1951. It is said that St Simon Stock composed the
hymn, *Flos Carmeli*.

> Flower of Carmel, vine with blossom weighed
> Shining light of heaven, bearing child though maid,
> None like to thee.
>
> Mother most tender, whom no man didst know,
> On all Carmel's children thy favour bestow,
> Star of the sea.

To the right of the reliquary altar is the chapel of the Carmelite
saints and in the centre, above the altar, is a medieval carving of
the Scapular Vision. On either side Kossowski has depicted rows
of friars and nuns turning towards the altar, in the manner of a
painting by Fra Angelico.

The last chapel I visit is dedicated to St Joseph and is dominated
by a magnificent statue of the saint by the sculptor Michael
Lindsey Clarke, who was responsible for the figures of the saints
over each doorway in the courtyard, and for the statue of Our Lady
in the piazza. His father, Philip Lindsey Clarke, one of the
country's foremost sculptors, was also responsible for the sculpture
of the Scapular Vision and many others. In describing the statue of
St Joseph, Michael Lindsey Clarke declared that he wished to
portray St Joseph with his feet firmly on the ground, giving an
impression of stillness and dependability.

Beyond the chapels and under a towering plane tree the lawns
run to the edge of the river, which is concealed by ancient brick
walls. Here is the Rosary Way where Adam Kossowski's mysteries of the rosary have been set in wooden frames in the manner of
a Polish shrine; on the day of my visit the air was heavy with the
scent of white and yellow roses.

As I sit and draw in the shade beside the Scapular shrine, beyond
the Rosary Way, the heat is almost unbearable. There is not a
breath of wind, and the stillness is broken only by the crunch of
wheels on gravel and the murmur of voices praying the rosary. The
voices fade and the sound of doves fills the air. I walk back along
paths skirting the outer walls of the chapels and notice that the
stained-glass windows appear from the outside to be composed of
a delicate lacework, as if this had been their sole purpose, and I
reflect as I prepare to leave that this unexpectedness is typical of
The Friars.

This is truly a place for people to experience, to walk around the grounds and the chapels, to come as a pilgrim of faith or of none, as each person becomes close to God in their own way. In this beautiful place, the holiness of Mount Carmel is open to everyone.

Canterbury

Aylesford was on the ancient pilgrim route to Canterbury, less than thirty miles away, a route that would have been familiar to Chaucer's pilgrims in the fourteenth century. The crypt shrine beneath Canterbury Cathedral was part of the rebuilding by St Anselm in the eleventh century, when an intricately carved Gothic screen was created to surround the original statue of Our Lady Undercroft. In 1982 a fine bronze statue of the Virgin and Child was carved for the Undercroft by the Benedictine sculptor Sister Concordia Scott of Minster Abbey in Kent. Her new statue restores an ancient shrine to Our Lady in one of the holiest places in the Christian world.

Shrine – Aylesford

LOCATION/ DIRECTIONS	From M25, exit J3 to M20 Exit J6 to A229, Follow signs to Eccles and The Friars By Train London Victoria to Maidstone East, taxi or bus to The Friars
CONTACT TEL. NUMBERS	The Friars Aylesford Kent ME20 7BX Tel. 01622 717272
EMAIL ADDRESS	enquiry@thefriars.org.uk
WEB SITE	www.thefriars.org.uk
TIMES OF SERVICES	MASS Sunday – 8.00am and 10.15am Weekdays – 7.30am and 12.00 noon
SPECIAL DATES/ EVENTS/ FESTIVALS/ PILGRIMAGES	Contact The Friars; most weeks there are Pilgrimages, Celebrations Concerts and Special Events
ROSARY GROUP	Weekdays at 6.30pm
ANGLICAN CHURCH AND CONTACT TEL. NUMBERS	St Peter and St Paul Aylesford Tel: 01622 719366 www.aylesford-church.freeserve.co.uk
LOCAL ATTRACTIONS	Shrine of Our Lady Undercroft in Canterbury Cathedral
GOOD PUBS	Tea Room on site
PLACES FOR PILGRIMS TO STAY	Guest House at the Friars

Shrine of Our Lady Undercroft

LOCATION/ DIRECTIONS	From M25, exit J2 M2/A2 to Canterbury Follow signs to city centre and Cathedral
CONTACT TEL. NUMBERS	Our Lady Undercroft C/o Canterbury Cathedral The Precincts Canterbury Kent Tel. 01227 762862
EMAIL ADDRESS	Enquiries@canterbury-cathedral.org
WEB SITE	www.canterbury-cathedral.org
TIMES OF SERVICES	Service held in The Chapel of Our Lady Undercroft Each Thursday at 3.30pm
RC CHURCH AND CONTACT TEL. NUMBERS	St Thomas 59 Burgate Canterbury Tel. 01227 462896
LOCAL ATTRACTIONS	Hales Chapel Hackington Kent http://www.digiserve.com/peter/hales-cf.htm
GOOD PUBS	Many bars, restaurants and cafés in city centre
PLACES FOR PILGRIMS TO STAY	Canterbury offers a wide selection of accommodation

2

Brewood

WHITE LADIES

Between Stafford and Wolverhampton lies the small town of Brewood. The Shropshire Union Canal runs through it and the Roman highway, Watling Street, passes to the north of this quiet and attractive place which is dominated by the tower and spire of the large Anglican church dedicated to St Mary and St Chad.

The size of the church in so small a town seems at first sight to be out of all proportion even to the aspirations of the most ambitious and eager clergyman. St Chad is responsible for this bold statement of faith, for when he was summoned in the seventh century from his beloved monastery in Lastingham to become Bishop of Lichfield, he found peace in this village.

The new Bishop preferred to walk rather than to ride, and in the two short years of his episcopate Chad covered great distances on foot within his diocese, spreading the Gospel wherever he went and talking to all whom he encountered. Although his home was amongst his monks in the monastery and church he had built in Lichfield, Chad frequently returned to Brewood.

In the year 672, one of Chad's monks was working in the fields when he heard the sweet sound of angelic singing and, lifting his head in wonder, he realized that it was coming from the little oratory in which the saint was praying. When questioned, Chad explained that the angels had come to summon him to heaven and that they would return in seven days' time. Gathering his monks around him, he exhorted them to lead good and holy lives, and on the seventh day the angels duly returned. The memory of St Chad is honoured in churches in the area and especially in Brewood.

Future bishops of Lichfield appear to have shared St Chad's fondness for the place, and during the thirteenth century it was decided that only a church of episcopal proportions would be appropriate.

Within the chancel of this beautiful church lie four tombs of members of the Giffard family; the women's dresses are delicately ruffled and the men are clad in armour. The finely-carved alabaster figures appear to be resting momentarily, for these are men and women of action, and their stories propelled this quiet backwater into the glare of history.

The earliest tomb contains the remains of the sixteenth-century Sir John Giffard. The keeping of exotic wild animals in private menageries was not unusual at the time and Sir John kept a panther at his home in nearby Chillington Castle. One day the panther escaped, whereupon Sir John and his son set out in pursuit and eventually discovered the animal stalking a woman carrying a child. Drawing his crossbow, Giffard shot the panther as it sprang and the place where the rescue happened was marked by an oak cross, known since then as Giffard's Cross. When news of this feat reached King Henry VIII, the family was rewarded with a crest emblazoned with an image of the head of the panther. Sir John died at the age of ninety and lies in Tudor armour beside his two wives, surrounded by the carved images of their eighteen children.

Queen Elizabeth I visited the next John Giffard in 1575, but this did not save him from many years' imprisonment for his Catholic faith. Despite a strong declaration of allegiance to the Queen when the country faced invasion by the Spanish Armada in the 1580s, Giffard forfeited his estates. He died in 1613 and lies clad in fine armour inlaid with steel.

In the north aisle there is a memorial plaque to William Carless and a copy of the Grant of Arms to him by King Charles II. Although Carless lies buried in an unmarked grave in Brewood churchyard, his association with Charles Giffard in 1651 provides the background to what is surely the greatest escape in English history; an escape which enabled the Catholic inhabitants of Brewood to practise their religion without fear of persecution and also led indirectly to the founding of the shrine of Our Lady of Brewood.

The Royal Escape

This corner of Staffordshire was once an area of almost impenetrable woodland, much of it belonging to the Giffard estate.

Deep in Brewood forest there stood a twelfth-century Augustinian priory which had been absorbed into the Giffard estates after the dissolution of the monasteries. This was a time of mixed feelings for Sir John Giffard. Sir John had prospered during the reign of King Henry VIII, having acquired considerable wealth through his own marriage and that of his son. He had managed to acquire several nunneries and other monastic properties as they lay empty and abandonded after their occupants had been expelled. Amongst these properties was the Augustinian priory of Whiteladies and the Benedictine priory of Blackladies at Brewood. When the Augustinian nuns departed, they left behind them an ancient wooden figure of the Blessed Virgin, which was treasured and cared for by the Catholic Penderels, tenants of the Giffards in the remote manor of Whiteladies. Surrounded by woodland and wildlife, the house and the ruins would probably have remained hidden from the public gaze had it had not been for the dramatic events of 1651.

At the first light of dawn on 4 September, a small group of horsemen in fear of their lives reached the forest of Brewood, having narrowly evaded their pursuers on the journey north. One member of the group had a price of £1,000 on his royal head, and among his companions was a member of the Giffard family on whose land they were to find temporary sanctuary.

This journey was the culmination of an enterprise which had begun in heady optimism. Eighteen months after the execution of King Charles I in 1649, his son, King Charles II arrived in Scotland from Holland, determined to reclaim the crowns of England, Scotland and Ireland. The royal party reached Worcester on 22 August with apparent ease. However, only twelve days later, on 3 September, the royalist forces suffered a decisive defeat at the hands of the Parliamentarians under Oliver Cromwell. Hundreds were left dead or wounded. Escape was vital if the king's life was to be saved, and Charles Giffard was among those who urged the King to flee with all speed.

As Catholics, the Giffards knew of a well-established network of safe houses, and were familiar with the vigilance and courage necessary in order to harbour Catholic priests and move them safely from one place to another. Such valuable knowledge was a priceless asset to the Giffards as they embarked on planning the king's escape.

As the dawn broke on 4 September Charles Giffard, with the small group including the King, headed initially for a Giffard hunting lodge, Boscobel House. Fearing for their safety, Giffard escorted the King and his companions deeper into the forest to Whiteladies, where the Penderels helped to disguise their sovereign. Richard Penderel lent his breeches, an old shirt and a pair of shoes. The shoes turned out to be excruciatingly uncomfortable and caused great distress to Charles, who could barely walk in them, and accounts of this great adventure are littered with tales of the bathing of the royal feet in different and dangerous venues. The royal hair was cut by Richard Penderel, and immediately after nightfall the group departed, heading for Wales. While the King had his feet bathed in vinegar, the Penderels learnt that government forces were searching every ferry and bridge that crossed the River Severn. In haste, the weary party returned to Boscobel, where many priests had found refuge.

At Boscobel the King met an old friend, William Carless. The Parliamentary forces were everywhere and Charles and Carless climbed into an oak tree which was to become famous as 'The Boscobel Oak'. The tree had recently been pollarded and therefore had a thick growth of leaves forming a bowl, in which the two hid for fourteen hours in incessant heavy rain. With bread and some beer to sustain them, Charles and Carless watched through the leaves as the Parliamentary troops searched the very ground beneath them. In the late evening the two clambered stiffly down from the tree and made their way to Boscobel House for supper.

The sovereign was then shown into a priest's hiding hole where he remained for the night. The hole was four foot square and Charles stood over six foot.

The following day news was received from the King's friend Lord Wilmot, who had been with him on his visit to Whiteladies. The King, accompanied by the Penderel brothers, hurried to join Wilmot at another Catholic safe house, Moseley Old Hall. It was here that he met Father John Huddleston, with whom he had long discussions about the Catholic faith. While at Moseley, Charles read a book written by Father Huddleston's uncle, the Benedictine Richard Huddleston, *A short and plain way to the Faith and the Church*, and took it with him when he left. When he lay dying thirty-four years later Charles sent for Father Huddleston, who once more prayed with him, anointed him and gave him Holy Communion before sending him on his final journey.

When word eventually reached the Parliamentary forces of the route taken by the royal party and of their brief stay on the Giffard estate, Whiteladies was ransacked and the building almost destroyed by fire. In the mêlée the wooden statue of the Blessed Virgin was badly damaged: the knee of the figure was pierced by a sword and a passing bullet lodged in the back. Shortly afterwards, the statue was taken for safe keeping to Blackladies in Brewood, the Benedictine nunnery acquired by the Giffards at the time of the Dissolution. Here the figure remained for over 200 years.

After numerous adventures, the King eventually escaped to France. Such was his gratitude that after his Restoration in 1660 he awarded pensions to the Penderel brothers and others who had taken part in his dramatic rescue.

Our Lady of Brewood

In 1844 the Giffards gave the land for a new Catholic church in Brewood. The building was designed by the architect Augustus Pugin in late thirteenth-century style with glorious stained-glass windows, three of which were donated by Pugin. A chapel had been established in the house at Blackladies in 1791 to serve the needs of local Catholics, and in 1887 the statue of Our Lady was taken from this chapel and placed on a stone altar in the Lady chapel of the new church, which is now known as the shrine of Our Lady of Brewood. The hole made by the Parliamentarian bullet is clearly visible and it is said that the wound on the knee of the figure occasionally weeps. Remarkable cures have been claimed by grateful petitioners.

Beside the altar in the Lady chapel a silk collage hangs on the wall, made by members of the parish and a seamstress from Stafford. On the wall beneath hangs an account of the shrine of Our Lady of Brewood by Peter Gosling, in which he describes the imagery of the different sections of the picture. Mary stands holding the document which gave the Catholics of Brewood the freedom to practise their faith without fear of penalty, in acknowledgement of the King's debt to the town. Although tacitly understood, the Deed of Immunity was not approved until April 1716, by which time George I was on the throne. The oak leaves recall King Charles II's sojourn in the Boscobel oak. The coat of arms of the Giffards is shown as a reminder of their gift of land for the church. There is a graphic image of the panther escaping from Chillington Castle, and of Sir John Giffard who saved the life of the woman and her child.

I came with other pilgrims to this beautiful church and, after the celebration of Mass and prayers before the shrine, we walked in the evening sunshine through the lanes to the Anglican church of St Mary and St Chad. We stood before the tombs of the remarkable Giffards and the nearby memorial to the King's friend, William Carless. For the rest of his life, Carless wished to be known as 'Carlos' in honour of the King he had served so bravely. How different the history of England might have been if Charles Giffard had not brought his exhausted sovereign to the forest of Brewood on that fateful night, less than twenty-four hours after the commencement of battle at Worcester. However, they found safety here as they hurried through the shadows of the manor of Whiteladies, passing the carved figure of the Blessed Virgin on their way.

The silk collage which hangs near to the statue includes the image of an acorn which is a reminder of the King's time spent in the oak tree, and also represents the growth of faith in this area. Two thriving churches bear witness to this. At the beginning of the third millennium they flourish and reach out to the community in the shared Christian charity of more peaceful times.

Shrine – Brewood

LOCATION/ DIRECTIONS	From M25, exit J16 M40, M42 North, M6, exit J10A M54, exit J2 A449 Stafford Road Follow signs for Brewood at roundabout Follow signs to Kiddemore Green Cross the canal bridge and St Mary is on the right-hand side
CONTACT TEL. NUMBERS	R.C. Church of St Mary Kiddemore Green Road Brewood, Staffordshire Tel. 01902 850394
EMAIL ADDRESS	father@stmarybrewood.org.uk
WEB SITE	www.brewoodvillage.org.uk Follow links on village website
TIMES OF SERVICES	MASS Vigil for Sunday: 6.00pm Sunday: 10.30am Holydays: 9.00am, 7.30pm
ROSARY GROUP	Thursday 7.45pm
ANGLICAN CHURCH AND CONTACT TEL. NUMBERS	St Mary the Virgin and St Chad Church Road Brewood
LOCAL ATTRACTIONS	Boscobel House and White Ladies Priory (English Heritage) Moseley Old Hall (National Trust) Tel. 01902 782808 Shropshire Union Canal; Countrywide Cruisers for narrow boat holidays based in Brewood Tel. 01902 850166, www.countrywide-cruisers.com
GOOD PUBS	4 good pubs in Brewood, 'The Bridge' is across the canal from St Mary's
PLACES FOR PILGRIMS TO STAY	The Blackladies Bed & Breakfast Brewood, Stafford, ST19 9BH

OUR LADY OF BUCKFAST

3

Buckfast

The entrance to Buckfast Abbey smacks of the twenty-first century as the visitor wanders past gift shops, ice cream stalls and the familiar paraphernalia of the tourist industry. A deafening peal of bells reminds one that this is a Benedictine enterprise; the sixth-century Rule of St Benedict interpreted for today extends a warm welcome to the thousands of visitors who arrive each year. In the rolling Devonshire country, midway between Exeter and Plymouth, Chaucer's pilgrims would have felt at home amongst these shops where anything from a straw duck to a rosary encourages weary travellers to part with their money.

At the heart of this great enterprise lies the monastic home of the monks of Buckfast and their magnificent abbey church. Benedictine monks originally arrived at Buckfast nearly a thousand years ago: the first known charter concerning Buckfast is dated 1018, and for over a century the life of the monastery was peaceful and largely agricultural. However, a spirit of renewal was abroad in the twelfth century, inspiring the foundation of new religious orders, and the creation of awe-inspiring abbeys.

In France, a stricter form of Benedictine life was being pioneered at the monastery of Citeaux under the guidance of an Englishman, St Stephen Harding, who was abbot for twenty-five years. His reforming work flourished when the young St Bernard arrived at Citeaux with his followers in 1112. This return to the letter of the Rule of St Benedict resulted in the foundation of numerous communities of Cistercian monks in England. Buckfast was not to be left out of this fervour and was refounded as a Cistercian monastery. In common with the others, it was placed under the protection of the Blessed Virgin.

The connection with Our Lady lasted until the mid sixteenth-century dissolution of Buckfast. Three hundred years later it was restored when the ruins of the abbey were bought for the sum of £4,700 by the French Benedictine community of La-Pierre-qui-Vire who had been exiled from France. Their arrival in 1882 was marked by the singing of the First Vespers of Our Lady and the dedication of this great enterprise to the Blessed Virgin.

There was considerable public interest in the return of the monks in 1882 and a committee was soon formed to help with the restoration of the abbey. Frederick Walters was appointed as architect, and restoration work started on one of the greatest monasteries of medieval England, using the few remaining ruins and a print showing the buildings as they had appeared in 1734. The work of restoration and repair has been unceasing.

After a few false starts, the original foundations were uncovered by a monk digging the garden. Gradually the perimeter of the original Cistercian monastery emerged and accurate drawings could at last be made, so that today's monastery stands on foundations laid in the twelfth century.

The work of restoration was planned by Abbot Boniface Natter who was later drowned at sea. Anscar Vonier, who had survived the shipwreck, was elected to succeed him and undertook the completion of the main body of the work in the early years of the twentieth century.

The story of the rebuilding is a remarkable tale of monastic ingenuity and several near disasters. The work was carried out by the monks themselves, and in old photographs they can be seen working on scaffolding some 150 feet above the ground, their habits blowing in the wind. There appears to have been no safety railing of any sort. One unfortunate monk, Brother Ignatius, fell fifty feet but his fall was broken by scaffolding and he then tumbled on to sand.

While the preparatory work was being carried out, the lower half of the original stone statue of the Blessed Virgin was unearthed. The architect, Frederick Walters arranged for the restoration of the figure, based on the design of an early monastic seal and the original colouring of the broken remains. This statue now stands in the Lady chapel of the abbey church, appropriately placed between two angels and beneath a window depicting the Annunciation. The remarkable achievement of Abbot Anscar is marked by a plaque on the south side of the sanctuary of the church in which he is shown offering his life's work to the Mother of God.

During the First World War much of the work of construction was still incomplete, and building materials were scarce to the point of non-existence. On one occasion, the monks turned to Our

Lady to ask for her assistance; the required stone duly material-
ized. It has since been the custom of the community to sing the
Memorare in the Lady chapel each evening after the office of
Compline in thanksgiving to Our Lady for her assistance.

Bees

A beautiful medieval garden has recently been created. A tunnel of
fruit trees when fully grown will form an intriguing entrance to this
little enclave beyond the abbey church, where the air is full of the
scent of flowers and the hum of bees. The garden is planted with
herbs and roses and there are secluded places in which to think –
or simply to sit.

Beyond the west side of the abbey there stands a life-sized statue
of the Blessed Virgin, set against tall hedges and surrounded with
all manner of lavenders, pink, white and deep blue; the scent is
overwhelming and the bushes are alive with bees. This outstanding
collection has been awarded National Collection status, but the
overriding purpose of the lavender is to provide for the Buckfast
bees.

For forty years one of the lay brothers, Adam Kehzle, travelled
the world in search of a disease-resistant and honey-producing
strain and finally bred the Buckfast bee. These bees are highly
productive and their sting is said to be far less aggressive than
those of other breeds, the effect, perhaps, of working in hallowed
surroundings. On his retirement in 1992, aged 93, Brother Adam
was recognized as a world authority on bee genetics and his work
continues at Buckfast today.

The Rule of St Benedict encourages suitable practical work
which can supply an income for the community; since 1897 the
monks of Buckfast have been highly successful in marketing their
tonic wine. Their endeavours also include the growing of vegeta-

bles, the husbandry of cattle and pigs – and of course bee-keeping.

There is an extraordinary atmosphere of old and new at Buckfast. I came on a Sunday in May and the bells were ringing out, drowning the cry of seagulls swirling about the abbey roof, a reminder that the sea is not far away. People were moving down the immaculately laid out grass paths towards the abbey church, young couples with arms entwined and older couples looking carefully to see where they were going. Some were lingering in the sun or sitting beside the statue of Our Lady amongst the lavender. Nuns in traditional habit walked past and disappeared into the church.

I had been sitting in the sunshine sketching a stone archway surrounding a door decorated with fine filigree ironwork; the door opened and a monk emerged, struck an arabesque, smiled at me and set off towards the abbey for the celebration of the community Mass. I followed his example and joined the congregation in the great abbey church.

BUCKFAST

Shrine – Buckfast

LOCATION/ DIRECTIONS	From M25 Exit J15 M4 Westbound M5 South A38 towards Plymouth Buckfast Abbey is well signposted on the A38 dual carriageway half-way between Exeter and Plymouth
CONTACT TEL. NUMBERS	Buckfast Abbey Buckfastleigh Devon Tel. 01364 645500
EMAIL ADDRESS	enquiries@buckfast.org.uk
WEB SITE	www.buckfast.org.uk
TIMES OF SERVICES	MASS Sundays 9.00am, 10.30am and 5.30pm Monday to Saturday 8.00am and 12.05pm Confessions, Saturday 5.45pm until 6.15pm
SPECIAL DATES/ EVENTS/ FESTIVALS/ PILGRIMAGES	Pilgrimages Beginning of May – Catholic Women's League Nearest Saturday to the Feast of the Assumption, 15 August The Knights of St Columba
ANGLICAN CHURCH AND CONTACT TEL. NUMBERS	St Luke's Buckfastleigh Devon Tel. 01364 644228.
LOCAL ATTRACTIONS	Dartmoor National Park; wild moorland, scenic walks and places of interest
PLACES FOR PILGRIMS TO STAY	Accommodation is available for groups. Those interested in making a private retreat can be accommodated at the abbey: male guests may stay in the monastery guest wing; male and female guests can stay in the Southgate retreat centre nearby

4

Caversham

CAVERSHAM

The pilgrims who visited this once-famous shrine across the River Thames to the north of Reading would be startled beyond belief by the approach to Caversham today. The lanes and byways which would have been familiar to the travellers of medieval England lie buried beneath motorways the width of two fields, and the cottages and inns that would have lined their route have been replaced by towering office blocks of steel and glass. Although the office blocks possess a certain beauty with sky and clouds reflected in their glass façades, a gentler world has been obliterated.

The approach to the modern shrine leads the pilgrim through a labyrinth of small streets into an oasis of peace. The restored shrine chapel stands beside the Church of Our Lady and St Anne, and the carved oak statue of the Virgin is set in perfect surroundings. There is even a slanted window by her side so that passersby may pause to greet the Blessed Virgin with a prayer without entering the church.

A mile away to the west is the site of the Saxon chapel dedicated in honour of Our Lady of Caversham. This is a place of lawns and cedar trees below the rise on which the twelfth-century Anglican parish church of St Peter stands above the River Thames. Stately swans glide silently past and fragments of ancient walls surround the area of the original shrine; the ruined cloister arches are now covered with ivy.

In 1162, the Earl of Buckingham founded Notley Abbey in Buckinghamshire for the Augustinian canons, and the church of St Peter in Caversham was included in the endowment. The Norman chapel dedicated to Our Lady of Caversham was obviously considered to be of sufficient importance to be named separately in the deed of gift to the Augustinian canons, and the transaction was confirmed by King John. Thus the shrine came under the care of the Augustinian canons, in whose hands it remained for over three hundred years.

The first written record of the existence of the shrine appears at the beginning of the twelfth century when Robert, Duke of Normandy, eldest son of William the Conqueror, returned from the Crusades with a relic of the Passion of Our Lord which he donated to the shrine.

The little chapel of Our Lady of Caversham may have been built by one of the many guilds dedicated to Our Lady. The guilds were forerunners to our trade unions and livery companies and were established with the three intentions of charity, friendship and prayer. The members of the guilds chose favourite saints to be their patrons and in Norfolk, of 909 guilds no less than 155 were dedicated to Our Lady.

The charitable work of the guilds frequently involved the building of chapels beside important and dangerous river crossings, and the shrine of Caversham was situated at one such crossing of the Thames. A chaplain to the guild would have been present at the chapel to pray each morning for the safety of travellers, and to point out the spiritual association between the journey of life and that of crossing the river with its unpredictable storms and moments of calm. It was the duty of those who crossed the river here to contribute towards the upkeep of the shrine.

The number of those wishing to cross the River Thames must have tested the oarsmen who plied to and fro, but they were soon to lose their trade altogether. Early in the thirteenth century the Benedictines of Reading Abbey built a bridge across the river at Caversham. The span of the bridge was so great that an island was formed in the centre of the river on which a small chapel was built. There was a well dedicated to St Anne in Caversham, and when the chapel on the bridge was completed this too was named in her honour.

The chapel has long since disappeared, and the well dedicated to St Anne has also vanished from the town. But the dedication is not forgotten: at the corner of St Anne's Road and Priest's Hill there is a strange Victorian structure over the place where the well once stood. Down the hill and across the new bridge, a plaque acknowledges: 'The little chapel on the great bridge 1231–1500'.

This chapel of St Anne on the island was much visited by pilgrims and contained the famous spearhead of which it was said that 'Angell with oon wing browt to Caversham. The spere hedde that peicyd Our Saviour his side upon the cross'.

The new bridge greatly improved the pilgrim route to the shrine of Our Lady of Caversham. The great and the good paused at the shrine on their way to fairs at nearby Reading and at St Giles in Oxford, and gifts of immense value were given to the Virgin in honour and in thanksgiving.

During the fourteenth century, the Lordship of Caversham passed by marriage to the le Despenser family. Isabel, the daughter of the ill-fated Thomas le Despenser who was beheaded for treason, married Richard Beauchamp and became Countess of Warwick. In 1439 she bequeathed to Our Lady of Caversham not only 'a crown of gold to be made from my chain and other broken gold in my cabinet, weighing 20 lbs' but jewels for the statue's crown as well. To give some idea of the importance of the shrine at Caversham, the same benefactor subsequently left to the shrine of Walsingham 'a tabernacle of silver, of the same timbre as that of Our Lady of Caversham'. This can leave us in little doubt of the opulence to be found here.

There are records of offerings made by King Henry VIII, and in a letter to Cardinal Wolsey written in 1532 from Easthampstead the diplomat Sir Robert Wingfield reports that: 'This morning the King rode forth right early to hunt and the Queen is ridden to Our Lady of Caversham'. This was the last visit that Catherine was to make to Caversham as Queen of England.

It is sad that those recounting these events saved their ink for the

OUR LADY OF CAVERSHAM

rich and famous; however, it is not difficult to imagine the bunches
of wild flowers picked from the hedgerows and the other small
presents from poor people who came to the shrine. The overall
picture that emerges was one of great wealth and luxury.

Dissolution

The chapel which had stood for five hundred years finally fell
victim to the reformers' zeal in July 1538. As the Dissolution ran
its course, it was inevitable that the value of the ornaments and
gifts at the shrine of Our Lady of Caversham should come to the
notice of that greediest of statesmen, Thomas Cromwell, and in
1538 the notorious 'visitor' of monasteries, Dr John London, was
despatched to dismantle the shrine. For all his terrible deeds, we
have to be grateful to Dr London for leaving us this graphic report
written for Cromwell at the time of the Dissolution.

> I have pulled down the image of your[sic] Lady at Caversham
> whereunto was great pilgrimage. The image is plated over
> with silver and I have put it in a chest fast locked and nailed
> up, and by the next barge that cometh from Reading to London
> it shall be brought to Your Lordship. I have also pulled down
> the place she stood in, with all other ceremonies, as lights,
> shrouds, crutches and images of wax hanging about the
> chapel.

Thus was all outward sign of the Catholic faith obliterated.

Across the river in Reading, the Benedictine abbey was almost
completely destroyed. The abbey had been founded by King Henry
I in 1121 and consecrated by St Thomas Becket in 1164. The last
abbot had formerly been a close friend of King Henry VIII and he
was acknowledged as a good and courageous man but this was not
enough to save him. Abbot Hugh Cook was executed as a traitor
at the gate of Reading Abbey in 1539.

The little chapel of St Anne on the bridge was closed and eventually became a private dwelling. When the old bridge finally had
to be replaced in the twentieth century, the foundations of the
chapel were unearthed. Some of the stone was placed in the
keeping of the Catholic parish priest until such time as it could be
used in any rebuilding work on the Church of Our Lady and St
Anne.

For three hundred and fifty years, the few remaining Catholics
of Reading and Caversham relied on the recusant strongholds of

Stonor and Mapledurham. This continued until 1896 when the first Mass since the Reformation was celebrated in Caversham.

On 1902 work began on a new church which was completed in 1933 and consecrated by the Archbishop of Birmingham. Mrs Crawshay of Caversham Park endowed the church with a high altar, organ and vestments. She also provided a fine white marble statue of the Virgin for the Lady altar and is considered by some to be the actual foundress of the restored shrine because of her great generosity.

During the Marian year of 1954 the decision was taken to build a special shrine attached to the church in honour of the Blessed Virgin. By happy coincidence, a medieval oak statue of Our Lady and the Holy Child had recently been acquired. The figure stands nearly five feet high, carved from a single piece of oak, and is believed to have been made in the Rhineland between 1480 and 1500. It is said that when the architect saw the statue he revised his plans for the shrine in order to reflect the importance of the figure. A new shrine has now been built and some of the ancient stone from the Chapel of St Anne on the bridge was placed in the walls. One is finely carved with the words 'JESUS MARIA'.

In 1996 the centenary of the first post-Reformation Mass in Caversham was celebrated with the crowning of the medieval oak statue of Mary. A crown of silver and gold was taken to Rome in May of that year to be blessed by Pope John Paul II. In July it was ceremoniously placed upon the head of the statue by the Papal Nuncio.

On the Sunday closest to the feast of the Annuciation in the year 2000 the town of Caversham was brought almost to a standstill by an ecumenical procession. Starting at the modern shrine, the pilgrims wound their way through the streets of Caversham to the site of the original chapel. This act of prayer has done much to heal the turmoil and dissension of four centuries. It brought with it a sense of hope for a future in which enmity may be forgotten and prayer may once more be said at the shrine of Our Lady of Caversham.

Shrine – Caversham

LOCATION/ DIRECTIONS	From M25 M4 Westbound, exit J11 A33 to Reading Central A329/A4155 to Caversham By Train Reading Train Station 0.5 miles
MAP	From Gosbrook Road turn north into Washington Road – left into South View Avenue.
CONTACT TEL. NUMBERS	Parish of Our Lady and St Anne The Presbytery 2 South View Avenue Caversham Reading Tel. 0118 947 1787
EMAIL ADDRESS	st.anne@virgin.net
WEB SITE	www.ourladyandstanne.org.uk
TIMES OF SERVICES	Saturday Vigil Mass – 5.30pm Sunday 10.00am and 6.30pm Holydays 7.00am, 9.15am and 7.30pm Weekday Masses are usually celebrated in the Convent Chapel Morning Prayer of the Church is said before 9.15am Mass Saturday 10.00am Mass in the Shrine Chapel
ANGLICAN CHURCH AND CONTACT TEL. NUMBERS	St Peters (on the bank of the River Thames) Church Road Caversham Tel. 0118 947 2729

LOCAL ATTRACTIONS	River Cruises, daily in the summer on the Thames to Henley (depart from Caversham Bridge) Tel. 0118 957 2388 Remains of Reading Abbey are in the Forbury Gardens in Reading town centre
GOOD PUBS	Pipers Island Alongside Caversham Bridge where the plaque for 'The Little Chapel' is sited
PLACES FOR PILGRIMS TO STAY	Contact: www.cavershamlife.org.uk

5

Chideock

CHIDEOCK

Chideock (pronounced Chidduck) in Dorset lies in the valley of the
River Winniford, surrounded by rolling hills and farmland stretching away into a blue haze and many of the thatched cottages in the
village are made from the local yellow sandstone of a quarry
nearby. The only blight on this idyllic scene is the thunderous A35
which cuts Chideock in two: calls for a bypass have so far fallen
upon deaf ears. For the visitor it is an area of beauty with a fascinating history.

On entering the village from the east, the road rises towards the fourteenth-century Anglican church of St Giles half-way up the hill on the right. The existence of a Christian community in Chideock goes back to the eleventh century, although there are no visible remains of the earliest church.

Turning down a small lane beside the church, I walked through the deep shade cast by the canopy of trees that line the route to Chideock Manor. Having failed to find the entrance to the Catholic church, I retraced my steps and found a small wrought iron gate near the manor. At the end of a narrow path beneath a tunnel of greenery the Italian façade of the church with its medallion of Our Lady surrounded by stars seemed almost ablaze in the evening sun. Even today, this hidden clearing is a reminder of the constant danger in which Catholics lived during penal times when concealment was vital and discovery could be a matter of death.

Chideock is famous for the martyrs who died here during the Reformation, and the beautiful romanesque church bears a dedication to 'Mary, The Immaculate Mother of God, and Queen of Martyrs, and St. Ignatius, Founder of the Society of Jesus'. Of the three hundred and sixty men and women who died for their faith during the sixteenth and seventeenth centuries, eight are known to have died either in Chideock or as a result of their labours in the area. Three of that number were members of the Society of Jesus.

During the reign of Queen Elizabeth I it was no longer possible for Catholics to worship at the church of St Giles. The story of the survival of Catholicism in this corner of Dorset centres around Chideock Castle which overlooked the village but has almost completely disappeared, so thorough was its destruction by the Parliamentary forces in 1645. Built in 1380 by John de Chideocke, the castle passed into the hands of the Lanherne branch of the Arundell family during the fifteenth century although Sir John Arundell continued to live at his homes in Muswell Hill in London and at Lanherne in Cornwall. Sir John was a renowned landowner, a staunch defender of the Catholic faith and his reaction to the passing of the 1549 Act of Uniformity, which outlawed the celebration of the Mass, was predictably defiant.

The ensuing persecution resulted in the death of countless priests and left Catholics without spiritual care. The search for replacement priests from abroad led Sir John Arundell to spread his net across the water to France. So successful was he that he and his successors ensured that Mass would be celebrated in the castle for nearly one hundred years. In times of extreme danger priest and people decamped to far-flung barns on the Arundell estates.

Amongst the protégés of this remarkable knight was John Connor O'Mahoney of Bodmin. Sir John sent this future Jesuit to study at Oxford, but his university career came to an abrupt end in 1578 when he was expelled for 'popery'. Having completed his studies at the English College in Rome, Father John Cornelius, as he was now known, joined his patron in London. With the death of Sir John Arundell in 1591 Lady Arundell moved to Chideock Castle and Father Cornelius became a member of her household and was active in the area for three years.

In 1594 John Cornelius was betrayed, together with two family servants, John Carey and Patrick Salmon. All three were arrested by the High Sheriff of Dorset, and as they were dragged away from the castle a relation of the Arundells, Thomas Bosgrave, offered Father John his hat. He too was arrested and shared the fate of Cornelius, Carey and Salmon.

While awaiting trial, John Cornelius was admitted to the Society of Jesus. The four men were in due course found guilty and sentenced to death. The three laymen were allowed to hang until dead, but Cornelius was cut down alive and suffered patiently the horrible butchery meted out to those convicted of high treason. All four bodies were later given honourable burial by the Arundells. Some fifty years later Blessed Hugh Green, the chaplain at Chideock, was arrested for being a priest and sentenced to death at Dorchester in 1642. John Jessop, Blessed William Pike and the Jesuit, Blessed Thomas Pilchard also worked in the Chideock area and suffered execution at Dorchester.

Chideock Castle was a Royalist stronghold during the Civil War, but was eventually captured by the Paliamentarians and demolished in 1645. Nothing remains of the buildings today, but at the east end of the village is a short track known as 'Ruins Lane' which leads to the place where a cross has been erected in memory of the Chideock martyrs.

The Welds

With the loss of the castle, the Arundells finally left the village and local Catholics were left to fend for themselves without a place of worship. For a hundred and seventy years a small barn on the site of the present church served as their meeting place.

At the turn of the eighteenth century the Chideock estate was in the possession of the eighth Lord Arundell of Wardour, who decided to sell in 1802. The barn in which the Catholics met was included in the sale, and the buyer was a Catholic cousin of the

Arundells, Thomas Weld. He gave the property to his sixth son, Humphrey, who built the present manor house and converted the barn into a small chapel. Humphrey's son and heir, Charles, was a gifted artist and a talented craftsman; in 1872 he transformed the chapel into the remarkable edifice we see today, and was himself responsible for much of the painting and decoration.

In such a country setting, one is unprepared for the extraordinary interior of the church with its strange mixure of the baroque, Gothic and Byzantine, and the remarkable gilded statue of the Assumption of Our Lady above the altar. There is a series of paintings of the Chideock martyrs by members of the Weld family; on one side we see Blessed John Cornelius, Blessed Thomas Bosgrave, Blessed John Carey and Blessed Patrick Salmon. On the opposite side, facing John Cornelius, is Sir John Arundell who was imprisoned but not martyred, and the Blessed Thomas Pilchard.

Charles Weld was prolific and covered walls, roof and dome with paintings of saints and angels, martyrs and cherubs. His work has recently been restored with the help of English Heritage, the Diocese of Plymouth, friends and parishioners and members of his family. The church contains precious relics, including fragments of the True Cross, the hair shirt of St Thomas More, and relics of the sixteenth-century Cornish martyr, St Cuthbert Mayne. Beside the church is a small and fascinating museum dedicated to the history of the village, and in particular to the history of the local recusant families who refused to attend the services of the Established Church. Crippling fines were imposed upon men and women who insisted on practising their Catholic faith and, when translated into modern currency, such sums explain the decline of many Catholic families.

On leaving Chideock Manor and its remarkable church, I walked back along the lane to the Anglican church of St Giles. Beneath the east window is the grave of Thomas Daniel, steward of the manor during the years of persecution who loyally defended the castle for his master, Sir John Arundell. Here again I discover the work of Charles Weld, in the form of a handsome carving of Christ crucified, on the wall of a small chapel. Beyond the church, the cemetery is divided by a wall which separates the tombs – Anglicans on one side, Catholics on the other. In this little cemetery the ornate graves bear silent witness, and in the gentle evening light the harsh divisions of history melt away in the numinous atmosphere.

Shrine – Chideock

LOCATION/ DIRECTIONS	From M25 Exit J12 M3 M27 Westbound A31 Dorchester A35 Bridport/Lyme Regis Chideock signposted 2 miles from Bridport on the A35 Turn right by St Giles Church $\frac{1}{4}$ mile along lane on right adjacent to Chideock Manor
CONTACT TEL. NUMBERS	Our Lady Queen of Martyrs and St Ignatius, Chideock Mrs Gaby Martelli Tel: 01308 488348 The Church is open daily between 10am and 4pm
EMAIL	amyasmartelli40@hotmail.com
WEB SITE	www.plymouth-diocese.org.uk/parishes/dorset/chideock.htm and www.chideockmartyschurch.org.uk
TIMES OF SERVICES	Mass every 3rd Friday at 6.00pm
SPECIAL DATES/ EVENTS/ FESTIVALS/ PILGRIMAGES	Pilgrimage on 4 July, Feast of the Martyrs (rotated within diocese) Visiting Pilgrimages between March and October are welcomed and are offered the opportunity to have history talks, information and booklets
ANGLICAN CHURCH AND CONTACT TEL. NUMBERS	Parish Church of St Giles Chideock Team Vicars with charge of Chideock; contact The Rectory, Charmouth. Tel. 01297 560409
LOCAL ATTRACTIONS	www.chideock.co.uk very informative village website Walks along the stunning Dorset coastal path
GOOD PUBS	The George, Main Street
PLACES FOR PILGRIMS TO STAY	Chideock House Hotel Main Street, Chideock, Dorset Tel. 01297 489242 www.chideockhousehotel.com

CLARE

6

Clare

The fields of Suffolk were shrouded in an early morning mist, the hedges and trees silhouetted against the weak autumn sun, as the road wound its way through the Stour valley towards the small town of Clare. Since the closure of the railways has cut this corner of Suffolk off from its neighbours, even the cars seem few and far between. In an area of vast skies and landscape stretching away into a haze of blue it is easy to understand why painters have been inspired by the extraordinary light here.

The houses of Clare stand back from the High Street, an elegant mixture of eighteenth- and nineteenth-century buildings edged by grass verges and an avenue of trees. Before the road arrives at the centre of the village, a sign points to Clare Priory. A lane edged with cob walls crosses the bridge over the river Stour and leads to the gate on which a sign announces that this is an Augustinian Priory (Austin Friars); founded 1248; suppressed 1538; restored 1953.

The drive winds beside the river and through woodland before opening on to the lawns which are studded with vast oaks and chestnuts. The priory is in part Tudor, with solid buttresses and gabled dormer windows rising up to its sweeping roofs; it stands, as it has for 750 years, comfortably settled in peaceful surroundings, the custodian of the history so concisely summarized by the sign at the gate.

One cannot help but wonder how the Augustinian friars first found their way from France to this hidden corner of Suffolk so many centuries ago.

When the first Richard de Clare came from Normandy to England in the train of William the Conqueror he was rewarded for his trouble with estates in Suffolk. One hundred and fifty years afterwards his descendant, Richard Earl of Clare, was approached by Cardinal Annibaldi, an emissary of Pope Innocent IV, who wished to find a suitable home for the first Augustinian priory in England. The de Clares were well known for their largesse towards the Church, and Richard readily gave the French friars this land in the shadow of his castle by the River Stour.

The priory at Clare became the first Augustinian foundation in the English-speaking world when the friars arrived in 1249 to make their home in what was to be their mother house in this country. The Order flourished, and by the time of the Reformation there were thirty-four Augustinian houses throughout England. From here the friars were to spread to Ireland and thence to America, Nigeria, Australia, Korea and Kenya.

From the beginning, the patrons of Clare Priory have been Our Lady, Saints Peter and Paul and St Augustine of Hippo. A shrine in honour of the Blessed Virgin was soon established, influenced in part by the de Clare family whose devotion to Mary played a large part in the foundation of other Marian shrines, including that of Our Lady of Walsingham.

On the day of our visit, we were accompanied by a friar who led us along a path edged with the last of the summer's Michaelmas daisies, towards the fourteenth-century cloister which is situated behind the main house. The first gateway was blocked by the tangled limbs of an ancient wisteria; we passed through the second arch, beneath a curtain of Russian vine, and into the cloister and garth planted with roses and lavender.

From there the path leads into more garden and orchard, the site of the original priory church built in the fourteenth century and dedicated to Our Lady in 1338. Surrounded by walls punctuated by the remains of pillars and arches, we were standing among fruit trees laden with apples and pears. The air was filled with birdsong. Within this enclosed orchard, half-hidden in deep grass, there lie the stone markings of the original Lady chapel which was added to the main church in 1361 and named in honour of the Annunciation. Across the lawns to the east there is a large stone altar, all that remains of the priory high altar, and here Mass is celebrated on special feast days. The remnants of the stone walls contain memorials to the de Clares, including Joan of Acre who married Gilbert de Clare in 1290.

Gilbert was forty-seven, some twenty years older than his bride who was a daughter of King Edward I. After giving birth to four children Joan died in 1307 at the age of 35. The memorial records that after her death, Joan was brought to the priory for burial and her brother, the future Edward II, attended her funeral in the absence of their father, who was leading his men into battle against the Scots.

Time seems to stand still in this serene and peaceful place and the atmosphere of the endeavours of the early friars is almost tangible.

Although the priory church gradually fell into ruin after the Dissolution, the gardens and orchards grew where friars had once chanted their prayers; a small plaque by the entrance records the dates of James Lewis who gardened here for forty years until his death in 1928.

As we retraced our steps, the friar accompanying us recounted the experiences of the Reformation at Clare Priory. During the years leading up to the Dissolution, some members of the community at Clare were apparently observing the Augustinian rule in a somewhat relaxed form. The prior joined the community at prayer only once a week. He ate with them on two days in the week – the minimum demanded by the Rule.

At first it seemed that Clare Priory would be exempt from the suppression of monastic houses, for several of their number co-operated with the King's chief minister, Thomas Cromwell, but the end was inevitable. In 1538 two separate campaigns suppressed all the remaining friaries in England and removed the shrines which had been so prominent in many monastic churches. At Clare many of the friars melted away into the local population. Some returned to France, from whence the community had come to Suffolk three hundred years previously. On 29 November 1538 the King's agent arrived.

Amongst the friars there were some who had already become enthusiastic Lutherans. The only one who refused to acknowledge Henry VIII as Supreme Head of the Church was Friar St John Stone and for this he was imprisoned by Thomas Cromwell. He was hanged, drawn and quartered on 17 December 1539 in Canterbury, on a mound still known as the Dane John mound, which originally took its name from the Norman-French word for castle, 'donjon', and is a lasting reminder of this brave man. In 1970 John Stone was canonized by Pope Paul VI as one of the Forty Martyrs of England and Wales. Today a statue of the saint, carved by Sister Concordia Scott of Minster Abbey, stands in the Martyrs' Chapel in the Catholic church of St Thomas in Canterbury.

Following the dissolution of Clare, King Henry VIII gave the priory to his trumpeter, Richard Frende, who complained loudly that the priory fell far short of the endowment he felt to be his due!

Renewal

Over the next few centuries, the buildings remained in private ownership. At the end of the Second World War, the house was owned by Helen May, the widow of Sir Henry May, who had inherited the property from her father Sir George Digby Barker. Fearing that the life of a rambling English country house would no longer be viable in the aftermath of two world wars, Lady May was anxious that the property should be returned to the original owners upon her death.

CLARE

Thus in 1953 the friars returned to Clare after an absence of some four hundred and fifty years. They found many of the original features of the priory unaltered and that little had been changed, apart from the addition of various outbuildings. Their return was welcomed by the local population, happy in the knowledge that Clare would once more be a place of prayer as in previous centuries.

A memorial to the family who lived in the house for so many years hangs on the remains of an ancient wall at the summit of the motte or castle mound. This is all that remains of Clare Castle, standing beleaguered but commanding views in every direction as far as the eye can see across the Suffolk countryside. From its base, a lane crosses the River Stour and leads through a small gate into the monks' cemetery.

Today the priory building is painted a startling pink which in its cheerful way dispels any sadness that might linger over the past and the visitor is immediately in the midst of a bustling parish and shrine. Across the lawns, beneath the chestnut trees, children run and jump as they throw sticks in the air in an attempt to shake conkers to the ground.

Beside the priory, there is an enclosed courtyard set beneath a sundial which hangs high on the chimney breast, marking out the passing of the hours. This is the little cloister with the chapel of Our Lady's shrine linked to the priory by a bleached oak passageway with its vaulted roof and low cob walls. The prophet Isaiah speaks of the Messiah as the Angel of Great Counsel and this shrine is dedicated to Mary, the Mother of Good Counsel.

The details of the image of Our Lady have been faithfully interpreted by Sister Concordia Scott. The ornate Orthodox haloes glow in an otherwise dark statue: the Holy Child grasps the golden collar of his Mother's dress and she leans her face towards him. The figure was installed and blessed at Clare in 1998 as part of the celebrations to mark the 750th anniversary of the arrival of the Augustinian friars in England in 1248.

The carving is suspended against blue and yellow walls above rows of candles and the words of the prayer to Our Lady of Good Counsel are printed for all to read, and to pray if they wish. On the Sunday after her feast day on 26 April, a procession takes place in the grounds of the priory.

Beside the statue is the small framed picture of the original fresco which inspired the carving of the shrine statue. This is a copy of the miraculous fresco which is in the keeping of the Order of St Augustine at Gennazano near Rome. According to legend, this image was taken by angels from Scutari in Albania, after its defeat by the Turks in 1467, and placed in the Augustinian church in Gennazano where it has been venerated ever since. When the friars returned to Clare in 1953 one of their number brought with him a framed copy of the fresco.

On the day of our visit we joined the families moving towards the church for Sunday Mass, passing through the long covered walkway to reach the priory church of the Mother of Good Counsel. It is a long and lofty cob walled building with sturdy buttresses and Gothic windows. This was once the community's infirmary, and the faint lines of the original upper floor can still be seen where there were once dormitories for the novices and their master. Although this beautiful church is far too small for the needs of today, the antiquity of the building makes alteration a daunting prospect. On the Sunday of our visit it reverberated with the music of guitar, clarinet and tambourine.

In the priory there is an unmistakable atmosphere of prayer, the hallmark of many religious communities, and here at Clare it is obvious that the laity contribute to this. The words of St Augustine sound urgently today: 'Be of one mind and heart on the way to God'. It is easy to understand the affection in which this place is held by those who come on retreat or to visit. Augustinian spirituality is timeless in its emphasis on the search for God in the midst of our everyday lives and in the inspiration it offers to the Christian desiring to engage with the modern world.

Under the direction of the prior, Father David Middleton, Clare is a place bustling with the life of a pilgrimage centre while retaining a calm and prayerful presence which is available to all. The shrine in honour of Our Lady, Mother of Good Counsel, offers those who come to this leafy corner of Suffolk an opportunity to experience the peace and happiness that is to be found in this beautiful place.

Shrine – Clare Priory

LOCATION/ DIRECTIONS	From M25, exit J27 M11 – exit J9 A11, A1307 and A1017 towards Haverhill/Braintree A1092 to Clare The Priory is along a lane on the right just before Clare town centre
CONTACT TEL. NUMBERS	Clare Priory Clare Sudbury Suffolk CO10 8NX Tel. 01787 277326
EMAIL ADDRESS	clare.priory@virgin.net
WEB SITE	www.clare-uk.com (town web site)
TIMES OF SERVICES	MASS Monday to Saturday – 10.00am Sunday – 8.00am and 10.00am Reconciliation: Any day after Mass
SPECIAL DATES/ EVENTS/ FESTIVALS/ PILGRIMAGES	Annual Pilgrimage – 2nd Sunday in May
ANGLICAN CHURCH AND CONTACT TEL. NUMBERS	St Peter and St Paul Tel. 01787 278501
LOCAL ATTRACTIONS	Clare Castle Clare Town Trail Antique Shops in Clare market town Long Melford 5 miles away
GOOD PUBS	The Clare Hotel
PLACES FOR PILGRIMS TO STAY	The Priory offers religious retreats, both day and residential

7

Coventry

I first came to Coventry on a grey December day and, with a heavy heart, drove through this once beautiful city, aware that the ravages of the Second World War had obliterated much of its history.

In its day Coventry was one of the jewels of medieval England, and a seventeenth-century visitor described the town as 'flourishing with fanes[temples] and proud pyramides'. When the novelist J. B. Priestley visited Coventry in 1933, he observed that 'much of the past, in soaring stone and carved wood, still remained in the city', and even the thriving post-First World War manufacturing industries did little to conceal the medievalism that still survived.

The bombing raids of the Second World War put an end to such romantic impressions. Although archaeologists and restorers have been working against time and against developers, the visitor is nevertheless greeted by houses, shopping malls and office blocks that were the accepted vision of the planners of the 1950s and 1960s.

There is a small area, surrounding Holy Trinity Church and the new cathedral, which is known as Hill Top. It stands on the low hill where much of medieval Coventry grew up. The narrow streets of fifteenth-century timber-framed houses, fine Georgian town houses nearby and the lawns across the way shaded by trees, are a breath of fresh air above the redeveloped shopping arcades and offices that encircle it. For a moment, in the cold winter mist of the December day, the sounds of history that linger on such still evenings seemed to fill the air. I could imagine Lady Godgifu and her husband Leofric, Earl of Mercia, emerging through the shadows of the eleventh century to visit their famous priory, the horses emblazoned with their livery.

In an omen of what would happen in later centuries, Coventry was already a scene of devastation when Godgifu and Leofric first set eyes on it at the beginning of the eleventh century. Coventry was so named because an ancient Saxon convent had existed here, founded by the Saxon abbess St Osburg. This now lay in ruins after a punitive raid by the Danes in 1016. At the suggestion of their confessor, Aefic, prior of Evesham Abbey, Earl Leofric and his wife founded a Benedictine priory on the site of the convent, in a surprisingly short space of time for a building of such magnificence. Leofric's charter for the priory endowed the foundation with lands in seven counties, sufficient to support an abbot with twenty-four monks. The charter was confirmed by St Edward the Confessor, who was so strongly in favour of the foundation that he freed the property from all taxation. The church became the most splendid in England, and the contemporary historian William of Malmesbury declared that people were dazzled by the unearthly, supernatural beauty of the interior.

The name Godgifu means 'gift of God' and Lady Godgifu was renowned for her holiness as 'the devout client of Mary' as well as for her beauty. However, she is more familiarly known to us as Lady Ghodiva or Godiva. In November 1043 the new priory was dedicated in honour of St Peter, St Osburg, All Saints and the Blessed Virgin. There is no record of the appearance of the statue of Our Lady at Coventry, but contemporary descriptions of the figures of the Blessed Virgin given by Godgifu to the abbeys of Ely, Evesham and Lincoln indicate her generosity, and we may presume that the statue she gave to Coventry was equally splendid. We know that Godgifu sold many priceless treasures in order to decorate the monastic church at Coventry. In his *Pietas Mariana Britannica*, the nineteenth-century antiquary Edmund Waterton tells us that she 'denuded' herself of her possessions, and one wonders whether this could have provided one foundation for the story of her famous ride.

Amongst her jewels Lady Godgifu possessed a particularly fine necklace which William of Malmesbury describes as 'a circle of threaded jewels upon which she was wont to number her prayers'. This was long before St Dominic could have 'invented' the rosary, and so it is safe to assume that the countess only used her jewelled beads to count her prayers; yet the instruction that her beads be bequeathed to the statue of the Blessed Virgin implies a devotion and gratitude for favours received.

This was an age in which men and women all over Europe were deeply aware of the role of the Blessed Virgin in the life of the Christian. Godgifu would have been amongst the many that turned to Mary as their mediator and recited the *Ave Maria* as well as the *Pater Noster* (the Hail Mary and the Our Father).

Leofric, Earl of Mercia, has had a mixed press, but during his lifetime he was one of the three great earls amongst whom the government of the kingdom was divided. Leofric was a loyal subject and a devoted husband. When he died in 1057 there is no doubt of the grief that was felt at the passing of so wise and generous a man.

The countess outlived her husband by ten years, during which time she experienced the Norman invasion of 1066, and saw her granddaughter widowed on the death of her husband King Harold at the battle of Hastings. Despite a life filled with good works, legend has obscured her gentle character.

More than a hundred years after her death, a tale was told of the day when Godiva rode naked through Coventry, clad only in her long golden hair. The story hinges upon an intransigent Leofric threatening to impose heavy taxation upon a people already crushed by poverty, and ignoring his wife's pleas on their behalf. In this somewhat unlikely scenario, Leofric agreed to lift the burden of taxation on condition that his wife would ride unclad through the city, certain, apparently, that Godiva's modesty would put any such expedition beyond the bounds of possibility.

Leofric reckoned without the depth of his wife's compassion for the overburdened populace. According to the legend, the people of Coventry hid behind shuttered windows in order to save her embarrassment as she rode through the town. The exception was a tailor named Tom, who peeped at Lady Godiva through the shutter of his window, and was struck blind: the origin of the phrase 'peeping Tom'. His part in the story is, however, a seventeenth-century embellishment in which Tom was apparently described as wearing clothes of the reign of Charles II. His effigy stands in Coventry's Cathedral Lanes shopping mall, and he is somewhat quaintly dressed as an Elizabethan soldier wearing a strange Napoleonic hat.

On the wall of a Georgian house which stands on the cobbled Priory Row leading from the ruins to the new cathedral, there is a plaque which reads: 'Leofric and Ghodiva are said to have been buried respectively in the two porches which stood nearly on this spot'. According to Edmund Waterton, the porch in which Lady Godgifu was buried was chosen for its proximity to the image of Our Lady.

After the deaths of Godgifu and Leofric, the priory was extended through the building of the Benedictine church, which was completed in 1220 and dedicated in honour of St Mary. The enlarged church measured some 425 feet in length and it is intriguing to walk the length of Priory Row today and to find the remains of the east wall of the Benedictine church immediately beside the new cathedral at the top of the hill: it gives one an idea of the immense size of the original building.

Henry VIII made a visit to 'our Ladye in the Tower at Coventry' in 1511 and left an offering, but within twenty years he had ordered the Dissolution of the monasteries and the great Benedictine church was demolished. For many years the ruins lay undisturbed. At the end of the seventeenth century the site was turned into a bowling alley and later became a garden.

The four flourishing trade guilds of Coventry were among the many institutions which disappeared during the sixteenth century; the guild hall of St Mary, beside the ruined cathedral of St Michael, stands on the site of the first hall built soon after the foundation of the guild in 1340, and was rebuilt at the turn of the fifteenth century.

Although the guilds had not been founded for specifically religious purposes, meetings often started with the celebration of Mass, and the guilds were most frequently founded in honour of the Blessed Virgin but also in honour of particular saints. Prayer was included in the statutes, and charitable duties were numerous.

The tradition of highly-skilled craftsmanship in Coventry undoubtedly stems from the trade guilds. Centuries later the craftsmen of Coventry dominated the car industry, and it was the existence of the Coventry armaments factories that drew the attention of German bombers during the Second World War.

Across the lane from the ruins of the priory stands the church of the Holy Trinity on land originally bequeathed by the Lady Godgifu. The church was built for the tenants of the priory and is one of the largest medieval churches in England. It is built in part from stone believed to have come from the priory.

Post Reformation

The original church of the Holy Trinity was highly decorated with painted walls, and numerous side chapels and chantry chapels in which Mass would be celebrated for the soul of a benefactor. Most of the paintings vanished over the centuries and an ambitious scheme is now under way to restore the doomsday painting on the magnificent ceiling.

When an incendiary bomb shattered the west porch of Holy

Trinity in 1940 a hoarding was placed over the gaping space on which a sage wrote the words 'It all depends on me and I depend on God' – words that were taken to heart by the intrepid vicar of Holy Trinity, the Reverend G. W. Clitheroe. Together with his son and his curate, Mr Clitheroe carried water, sand and hawsers on to the roof of Holy Trinity and there the three men slept, night after night, throughout the blitz, guarding the fine roof of the church.

Lady Godgifu also left the land on which the church of St Michael was built for the people of Coventry, and this was promoted to cathedral status in 1918. On a clear moonlit night in November 1940 the inconceivable happened, and this magnificent building was almost completely destroyed by the Luftwaffe, save for its fine tower and a few walls.

The tall pink and grey stone walls of the new cathedral rise like some latter-day Goliath beside the ruins of St Michael's Church. In its austerity, the new cathedral is a severe reminder of the tragedies of the twentieth century. Thin shards of stained glass filter light across its cold nave, and yet the glass engravings of the angels and saints by John Hutton on the east window are a ghostly whisper of joy that Coventry has once more risen from the ashes.

The Catholic church of the Most Holy Sacrament and St Osburg, dedicated in 1845, was named after the Saxon abbess on whose land Godgifu's priory had been founded. This Gothic stone church was built by William Ullathorne, Benedictine monk of Downside Abbey, and subsequently the first bishop of Birmingham in 1850 when the Roman Catholic hierarchy was restored. To assist him in this great building programme, Father William turned to Margaret Hallahan, the foundress of the Dominicans of Stone, who was to play such a pivotal role in the shrine of Our Lady of Stone. Margaret had been professed as a Dominican in Bruges and brought to England with her the statue known as Our Lady, Refuge of Sinners, which was carried in public procession in Coventry in 1842, the first public procession of this sort to be held in England since the Reformation. The work of restoring Catholic life in Coventry was immense. The young women who assisted with it were to form the foundation of the Dominican Sisters of Stone.

The Benedictines of Douai Abbey cared for St Osburg's Church until 1992, when Father Patrick Kilgarriff arrived as parish priest. It was among his earliest duties to preside over the committee that had been formed to revive the shrine of Our Lady of Coventry. Sister Concordia of Minster was commissioned on behalf of the Catholic community to create a statue which was to be based on

REMAINS 11c
CATHEDRAL PILLARS
COVENTRY

the original seal of the priory. The statue was to be their gift to the city of Coventry to mark the millennium but no decision had been taken on its eventual resting place.

Upon its arrival in Coventry, the bronze statue was taken on tour around the local Catholic parishes in acknowledgement of their gift. With the agreement of the city council and the cathedral authorities it was placed within the recently excavated nave of the priory ruins. The ceremony was held in Coventry Cathedral on 11 March 2001, attended by 2,500 people, including the Bishop of Coventry and many ecumenical and civic guests. Monsignor Patrick Kilgarriff returned from Rome where he was now Rector of the English College in order to preach at the service. In a fine spring drizzle, the procession bearing the statue left the nave of the cathedral for the nave of the original priory.

The ability of this unique city to survive and revive against overwhelming odds is reflected in the Millennium Project, aptly named The Phoenix Initiative. This ambitious plan to excavate the foundations of the original priory church attracted the attention of Channel Four's 'Time Team' who undertook the initial dig. This project and, at the same time, the plan to restore the shrine of Our Lady of Coventry were unrelated, and yet both undertakings have now been triumphantly completed. It is now possible to visit the revealed remains of the building that was a wonder of the medieval world, and at the same time, to see in the nave of this great priory church, the bronze statue of Our Lady of Coventry. Once again, she is seated with the Holy Child on her lap and a Saxon crown upon her head.

The bronze statue carved by Sister Concordia of Minster Abbey reflects the wish of Lady Godgifu that her fine jewelled necklace should be 'hung about the neck of the Blessed Virgin's image in the church at Coventry'. Every Saturday evening since its restoration, a group of people has gathered before the image of Our Lady of Coventry in the priory ruins to count their beads in prayer as Lady Godgifu, Countess of Mercia, counted her beads nearly a thousand years ago.

Shrine – Coventry

LOCATION/ DIRECTIONS	From M25, exit J16 M40, exit J15 A46 to Coventry A4114 to city centre Head clockwise on ring road and exit J5 Leave roundabout head for New Union Street Turn right into Little Park Street and left into St Mary Street Left into Bayley Lane, right into Cuckoo Lane and finally left on to Priory Way Holy Trinity is next door to Coventry Cathedral, adjacent to Priory Gardens, opposite the Allder's department store in Broadgate, close to the statue of Lady Godiva and the famous Peeping Tom Clock.
CONTACT TEL. NUMBERS	The shrine statue is in the newly-excavated remains of the twelfth-century monastery, immediately opposite the Holy Trinity Church (St Osburg is approximately a 20 minute walk from the shrine) Roman Catholic Church of The Most Holy Sacrament and St Osburg Upper Hill Street Coventry CV1 4AQ Tel. 024 7622 0402
ANGLICAN CHURCH AND CONTACT TEL. NUMBERS	Holy Trinity Church 5a Priory Row Coventry CV1 5EX Tel. 024 7622 0418 www.holytrinitycoventry.org.uk
LOCAL ATTRACTIONS	Coventry Cathedral, 7 Priory Row, Coventry CV1 5ES www.coventrycathedral.org www.historiccoventry.co.uk excellent website with local history and information The Herbert Art Gallery and Museum, Jordan Well, Coventry Free Admission
GOOD PUBS	Many places to eat and drink in city centre

| PLACES FOR PILGRIMS TO STAY | Coventry Tourist Information Centre
Bayley Lane
Coventry
Tel. 024 7622 7264
www.visitcoventry.co.uk |

DONCASTER

8

Doncaster

'Just follow the signs to the racecourse', a kind Irish voice came down the telephone line, and I recognized at once that irresistible lure of the horses that draws the holiest of Irish priests. The instruction could hardly have been more accurate and, sure enough, the road turns just beside the racecourse and within a few hundred yards there I can see, above rows of terraced houses, the crown that surmounts the Catholic church of St Peter in Chains.

The tragedy that tore Christendom apart in the sixteenth century and resulted in the destruction of the shrine of the Blessed Virgin in Doncaster became painfully obvious as soon as I arrived at St Peter in Chains. Immediately opposite this new and imposing Catholic church stands a fine Victorian Baptist church. The ancient shrine of Our Lady of Doncaster is restored in the Catholic church but our separation from other Christians remains.

The Reforming Bishop of Worcester, Hugh Latimer, wrote to Thomas Cromwell concerning the statue of Our Lady of Doncaster amongst others, so determined was he to put an end to the England in which men and women travelled on pilgrimage, enjoying the fun of a gathering as well as offering prayers at these much-loved shrines.

Latimer's efforts were rewarded with success and most of the statues from the shrines he listed were burnt, that of Doncaster among them. Now, long after his memory has faded in this area, people are coming once more on pilgrimage to Our Lady's shrine.

Original Foundation

The origins of the shrine of Our Lady of Doncaster stretch back to the fourteenth century. Under the patronage of King Richard II, and his uncle John of Gaunt, Duke of Lancaster, the Carmelite foundation at Whitefriars in the heart of the town was granted a licence in 1350 to build a church in honour of the Blessed Virgin with living quarters nearby. Doncaster, with its fine priory and the shrine of Our Lady, soon became a popular stopping-place for royalty on their way from London to the north.

Henry VII stayed overnight on his progress north after his coronation and attended Mass in the shrine the following morning – a visit of note for the people of Doncaster, as Henry's reign brought an end to the rivalry between the Houses of York and Lancaster with his marriage to Elizabeth of York. Doncaster was very much a Yorkshire shrine.

Through his mother Margaret Beaufort's great-grandfather John of Gaunt, Henry inherited the Lancastrian claim. Some years later, Henry's daughter Margaret also stayed in Doncaster en route to her wedding to King James of Scotland.

The fame of the shrine of Our Lady of Doncaster increased after a miracle was reported early in the sixteenth century. Robert Leche, his wife and two children, set out to cross the River Don in a wagon drawn by six oxen and two horses. Hardly had the group set out than a storm blew up, waves battered the wagon, and the passengers were assailed by wind and rain. The wagon was upended and the lead horse drowned as they were swept downstream. Each in turn called in distress on Our Lady of Doncaster, and eventually they were all saved, with the apparent exception of Robert Leche's wife, who had been trapped beneath the wagon as it crashed over the rocks. Those who had clambered to the bank fell on their knees and prayed for this poor woman, and after what seemed an eternity, she too struggled to the bank and emerged unscathed. On the feast of St Mary Magdalen, Robert and his family came to Our Lady's shrine to give thanks and to declare that this was indeed a miracle.

Thirty years later, the looting of churches and monasteries by the agents of Cromwell had become a familiar sight, and a general sense of unease developed into open revolt in 1536 when the people of Louth in Lincolnshire rose and seized the city of Lincoln. Flushed with success, the movement gathered strength and spread across the northern counties. Amongst their number was a country lawyer named Robert Aske, who is remembered for the bravery of his part in a more determined protest which followed in Yorkshire and became known as the Pilgrimage of Grace.

On an October day in 1536, on the banks of the River Don, the chivalry of northern England stood beneath the banner of the Five Wounds of Christ: some 30,000 men, an army almost four times the size of the King's army that was sent to meet them.

The scars left by this tragedy took generations to erase from memory, and in some people they linger to this day. These men of the north were peaceful countrymen who, when called upon, guarded England against the Scots. They looked with awe on the monasteries so willingly endowed by their ancestors, the places in which their fathers were buried and where they themselves had been educated.

They turned to the monks and abbots for advice as trusted counsellors and wise friends in all the vicissitudes of their lives. These holy and dependable pillars of their world were being wrenched from them, bringing to an end a way of life that had endured for four centuries. It was a matter of honour that a stand should be taken in defence of their faith against their enemies and the enemies of the King. Thus it appeared to those who gathered under the leadership of Robert Aske on the edge of the River Don that October day in 1536.

Who knows what might have happened if battle had taken place? Instead Aske dispersed his great army on the King's promise of a general pardon and a Parliament to be held in York within the year. In less than six months, Aske and forty-six of his companions had been executed and the gibbets stood thickly in every part of Yorkshire. So ended the Pilgrimage of Grace, and whatever the wrongs of the monasteries, real or imagined, nothing could justify the vengeance wrought against a quixotic and noble protest.

While the tragedy unfolded, Robert Aske made his headquarters here in Doncaster, at the Carmelite house at Whitefriars in the heart of the town. As the King's promises evaporated, the Carmelite prior Laurence Cooke was among those arrested and taken to the Tower of London under sentence of death. He was still imprisoned when Cromwell himself fell from grace and was executed in 1540. Prior Cooke was pardoned the following October, but it was too late; he had been beheaded in August.

The statue of Our Lady of Doncaster had already been removed by Latimer from the shrine of Whitefriars where it had stood since its founding some two hundred years previously.

Royal visits, miracles and pilgrimages had been part of the life of the people of Doncaster. With the Dissolution and disappearance of the shrine all was swept away and silence descended on a once bustling part of the town.

A new shrine

There was a move towards restoring a Catholic parish in Doncaster
in 1833, and within two years there was a resident priest. The
church was opened in 1855, dedicated to St Peter in Chains, and a
few years later a Lady chapel was added.

No record of the appearance of the original statue of Our Lady
of Doncaster could be found and Father Pearson, the parish priest,
therefore gave detailed instructions to the sculptor Phyffers in
London. The design is fifteenth-century and English in character,
with Our Lady holding the Holy Child on her left arm. The Child
holds on to his mother's veil as in many fourteenth- and fifteenth-
century statues, and carries an orb in his left hand. Although he is
barefoot, the Virgin is wearing shoes, as in many early Byzantine
figures. The hand which holds the Child is open, as if to gather the
prayers of those who turn to her and which she will hand to her
son.

The statue now stands in the new church which was opened by
the Archbishop of Westminster, Cardinal Heenan, in 1973. The
congregation had outgrown the original building as the local population increased and the number of Catholics grew. It is an imposing octagon, flooded with light, but the arrangement of the space
in which the congregation is seated turns the celebrant's task of
preaching into a neck-swivelling exercise reminiscent of a tennis
umpire. The shrine chapel stands on the north side beneath stained
glass windows depicting St Joseph, the Annunciation, the Nativity
and the Assumption of Our Lady.

An archway in Priory Lane reminds one of the Carmelite friary
of Whitefriars that once stood on this spot. On a warm July day
we walked through the streets of Doncaster to the pedestrianized
area which is filled with flowers and lollipop-like metal trees, until
we reached Priory Lane. On either side of the arch there hang two
shields decorated with the three stars of Our Lady of Mount
Carmel, and in the nearby pedestrian area three silver stems
emerge from the ground, each with a star-like flower.

As we stood there, a young man walked through the archway,
his face and ears pierced with studs and rings, his head topped with
startling orange hair arranged in spikes. I noticed on his T-shirt the
words 'Jesus is coming' beneath an image of the cross, and the
additional slogan 'Be prepared'. Amongst the rest of us so plainly
clad, this man alone might have felt at home with the medieval
pilgrims who came to this renowned centre of prayer, some of
them no less exotically clad.

DONCASTER

In a contemporary church we had found an ancient shrine whose history is closely associated with events in Yorkshire history, including the Pilgrimage of Grace, which are for the most part forgotten. But the bravery of those who took part in an ultimately-doomed effort to preserve the original shrine and many more like it has not been wasted. The revival of the shrine of Our Lady of Doncaster in more peaceful and ecumenical times is hardly surprising in the light of the determination of the people of Yorkshire.

SAINT PETER IN CHAINS

DONCASTER

Shrine – Doncaster

LOCATION/ DIRECTIONS	From M25, exit J21, M1 Exit J32 M18 Exit J3, A6182 Doncaster Turn right at roundabout into Carr House Road Turn 2nd left into Cunningham Road Turn right into Apley Road Turn left into Chequer Road
CONTACT TEL. NUMBERS	Roman Catholic Church of St Peter in Chains Chequer Road Doncaster Tel. 01302 342068
EMAIL ADDRESS	doncaster@catholicweb.com
WEB SITE	www.doncaster.catholicweb.com
TIMES OF SERVICES	MASS Sunday 10.00am, 1.15pm, Polish 6.00pm Monday 7.00pm Tuesday No Mass Wednesday 12.15pm Thursday 10.00am Friday 12.00 noon Maridon Centre, Netherhall Road
ROSARY GROUP	Rosary every day after Mass Tuesday 7.30pm
ANGLICAN CHURCH AND CONTACT TEL. NUMBERS	St Mary's Church St Mary's Road Wheatley Doncaster www.stmaryswheatley.org.uk
LOCAL ATTRACTIONS	Doncaster Racecourse (1 mile away) www.doncaster-racecourse.com Museum and Art Gallery Chequer Road Doncaster www.doncaster.gov.uk/museums
GOOD PUBS	Many pubs, cafés, restaurants in town centre

| PLACES FOR PILGRIMS TO STAY | Doncaster Council (contact for list of accommodation) 2 Priory Place, Doncaster, DN1 1BN Tel. 01302 734444 www.doncaster.gov.uk |

9

Evesham

EVESHAM

This small Worcestershire market town lies at the heart of 'the orchard of England' where once there stood the greatest abbey in the Anglo-Saxon kingdom of Mercia. The approach to Evesham from the east descends steeply from the wooded hills of the Cotswolds to the plateau of the Vale of Evesham, and the town stands in a loop of the River Avon. Across the vale, the orchards with their neat rows of fruit trees cover the landscape like lines of guardsmen.

On entering the town, the road leads past a handsome group of medieval buildings. Across a grass sward stand two twelfth-century churches beside the ancient timbered gatehouse. To the right and beyond these buildings is the fourteenth-century Heritage Centre and Museum, known as the Almonry, and once the home of the abbey almoner who cared for the poor and welcomed visitors. Beyond is Abbot Lichfield's bell tower, standing alone since the sixteenth century when it replaced an earlier bell tower destroyed by lightning. These are the only remnants of the third largest abbey in England; the great abbey of Evesham in which a shrine in honour of the Blessed Virgin stood for nearly eight hundred years.

The story of the founding of the abbey and the naming of the town itself is illustrated with almost childlike simplicity on the thirteenth-century Evesham abbey seal which can be seen today in the Almonry.

The picture on the seal illustrates the story of Eoves, a swine-herd, who was blessed with the vision of a beautiful maiden accompanied by two attendants. Beside Eoves are the words:

> Eoves her wonede ant was swon,
> For thi men clepet this Eovisham

> Eoves dwelt here, and his swine,
> Therefore men call this Evesham

On the seal, Eoves appears to be looking up at the vision of the Virgin amongst the trees; overwhelmed by her beauty, Eoves hurried off to tell Egwin, his bishop, who came to see for himself. Egwin also saw the Virgin just as Eoves had described her. She blessed the bishop with a golden cross, uttering the words 'This is the place I have chosen'.

A small church was duly built by Bishop Egwin, who soon abandoned his bishopric to begin building an abbey in which the Benedictines were to be installed. Evesham is said to have been the only monastery in England founded at the express wish of the Blessed Virgin and it was dedicated in her honour.

Despite his holiness, or perhaps because of it, Egwin had enemies and in the year 700 he travelled to Rome to explain to Pope Constantine the injustice of their accusations. Before setting out, Egwin attached shackles to his ankles as an act of penance and threw the key into the River Avon, trusting that in the good Lord's time the key would in some way be restored to him.

On reaching Rome, he celebrated Mass at the tomb of St Peter, and later dined on a fish that had just been caught in the River

Tiber. Legend has it that the fish had the key to Egwin's shackles in its stomach, and as news of this miracle travelled through Rome, his prestige was restored. On his return to Evesham, Egwin adopted the image of the bolt and shackle as the abbey coat of arms. A carving of this can be seen today in the entrance to the Anglican parish church of All Saints.

After a life of vicissitudes, Egwin eventually found peace and was buried at the foot of Our Lady's shrine and came to be regarded as a saint. His little church stood for some two hundred years before finally falling down in 960. For fifty years the ruins remained undisturbed until Leofric, Earl of Mercia, and his Countess Godgifu or Ghodiva, came forward to build a new church for the abbey at the beginning of the eleventh century.

From all that we know of the munificence of Earl Leofric and his wife, we can imagine the probable splendour of the church. But within fifty years this too was to be replaced. With the arrival of the Normans after the Conquest, building started in 1077 on the great abbey of Evesham, and this was still incomplete at the time of the Dissolution four hundred years later.

The abbey and shrine of Our Lady of Evesham drew pilgrims from all over Europe, and in keeping with ancient custom, candles burned day and night in front of the Lady altar in the crypt.

Two additional churches were built which stand today: the church of St Lawrence, and the church of All Saints.

The church of St Lawrence was built to care for the spiritual needs of the crowds who thronged to Evesham, while the church of All Saints was built as a parish church to cater for the needs of the local community. Both remain long after the disappearance of their sister church, the great abbey. In the 1970s the church of St Lawrence was declared redundant after the failure of many attempts to restore it. St Lawrence's is now maintained by the Churches' Conservation Trust, and its many treasures include a stained-glass window in the north aisle which illustrates the story of Eoves and his vision.

The Heritage Centre or Almonry houses a Bible in which notes were found that had been written by a monk at the time of the Dissolution. He describes the arrival of the commissioners' soldiers on a Friday evening in 1540 during the singing of Vespers. The monks never sang in the abbey church again. It was completely destroyed.

Only the forlorn vestiges of ancient walls and arches remain today. There is a cloister arch with carved figures of the saints bearing traces of the Reformers' destructive zeal; few have heads left on their shoulders, as if such damage would remove any temptation to honour the saints. The perimeter wall is all that remains of the cloister, and the central ground is now given over to extensive kitchen gardens; this seems most appropriate in view of the importance given to manual work in the Rule of St Benedict, which would have been followed by the monks of Evesham.

The outline of the abbey and chapter house are clearly marked with stones laid out in the grass of the park that leads down to the river. Close to the bell tower is a memorial to Simon de Montfort, Earl of Leicester, the father of the English Parliament. De Montfort was killed at the Battle of Evesham in 1265 and the grieving monks recovered his body and brought it for burial in front of the high altar of the abbey church. Beyond the park the hill descends past the remains of the old abbey fish ponds to the River Avon. The Hampton ferry plies the crossing in the summer, as it did so many centuries ago when the monastery flourished.

The appearance of the original shrine statue of Our Lady of Evesham is unknown, but a short journey to the village of Fladbury nearby reveals a remarkable medieval panel in the church of St John the Baptist. This is a beautiful church with fine stained glass, and the illuminated panel is contemporary with the completion of the abbey church and depicts Our Lady and the Holy Child. In the Heritage Centre a small seal bears a striking resemblance to the panel in Fladbury church which strengthens the possibility that the panel in the church was perhaps copied from the original statue of Our Lady depicted on the seal.

It was not until the beginning of the twentieth century that a Catholic priest once more took up residence in the town. Father Patten arrived in Evesham in 1900, and set about building a new church which was completed in 1913 and dedicated to St Mary and St Egwin, the latter having built the first church. It is a fine building with delicate screens on the main altar and in the Lady chapel. At the entrance to the church is a small statue of the Blessed Virgin carrying a small cross – a reminder of the way in which she was once described by Eoves. Displayed on a kneeling bench beneath the altar in the Lady chapel is a copy of the prayer of Our Lady of Evesham written by Father Arthur Proudman who was parish priest at the time.

In 1952, the first public procession was arranged, and is now an annual event, taking place on the second Sunday in June. The statue of Our Lady of Evesham is carried from the Catholic church, along the High Street and into the abbey grounds. Of the many people of all denominations who join this pilgrimage, there is amongst them a Benedictine monk, the titular abbot of Evesham from Douai Abbey.

Shrine – Evesham

LOCATION/
DIRECTIONS

From M25, exit J16
M40, exit J15
A46 Evesham
Follow signs for Railway Station and into High
Street
Church parking restricted

CONTACT
TEL. NUMBERS

Roman Catholic Church of Our Lady and St Egwin
118 High Street
Evesham, Worcestershire
Tel. 01386 442468

TIMES OF
SERVICES

MASS
Monday to Thursday 10.00am
Friday 7.00pm
Saturday 11.00am
Sunday 8.00am, 10.00am and 6.30pm

SPECIAL DATES/
EVENTS/
FESTIVALS/
PILGRIMAGES

Annual pilgrimage held 2nd Sunday in June
Parish pilgrimages can be arranged, please
phone first

ROSARY GROUP

Rosary, said after the 10am Mass
Wednesday evening, Eucharist service and rosary
7–8.00pm

ANGLICAN
CHURCH
AND CONTACT
TEL. NUMBERS

All Saints
Market Place
Evesham
Tel. 01386 442213

LOCAL
ATTRACTIONS

Almonry Heritage Centre and Museum
(also Tourist Information)
Tel. 01386 446944
Abbey Park (remains of Abbey)
Stratford on Avon 15 miles away to the south
Cheltenham 15 miles away to the north-east

GOOD PUBS

Many pubs, cafés and restaurants in town centre

PLACES FOR
PILGRIMS TO STAY

Contact Tourist Information at the Almonry

LADYE WELL

10

Fernyhalgh

The shrine of the Blessed Virgin at Fernyhalgh (pronounced ferny-huff) is hidden in the depths of Lancashire to the east of Preston. The journey leads through a labyrinth of tortuous and remote country lanes and one is aware of the roar of traffic on the M6 a quarter of a mile to the west.

A small sign points down Fernyhalgh lane, and I find myself standing before a large plain building that, on closer inspection, turns out to be a church dedicated in honour of Mary. As yet, there is no sign of a shrine. I open the door and enter, entirely unprepared for the extraordinary interior that awaits me.

The almost Byzantine decoration surrounding the altar glows in the autumn sunlight filtering through the stained glass, creating an atmosphere that woud be more familiar in Italy than in the depths of Lancashire.

So far there had been no sign of life in any shape or form, and I had not passed anybody on the final stages of my tortuous journey. With my spirits falling, I realised that there was no evidence of the holy well.

Turning to leave, I found that I was no longer alone. A man had entered the church silently and was standing, rosary in hand, obviously anticipating my questions. He urged me to continue on down the lane, assuring me that despite the impression it gave of leading nowhere, it would in fact take me to the well and to the shrine of Our Lady which both lay beyond the trees.

Some 300 hundred yards further down the lane, across a cattle grid and hidden by towering trees, there stands a white house. In the garden is a statue of the Madonna and Child beside a deep well. The overwhelming silence of the place is broken only by the song of birds and there is an awareness of standing on hallowed ground.

The origins of Ladyewell are recounted in detail by Father

Christopher Tuttell, sometimes spelt Tootle, missionary priest at Fernyhalgh from 1699 until 1727. He set the date of its foundation as 1471, although other writers claim that Ladyewell goes back to the twelfth century. Whatever the truth concerning the date, the details of the legend do not differ.

The Apple Tree

A wealthy and respected Irish merchant, Fergus Maguire, the son of a Chief of Fermanagh, was sailing across the Irish Sea when a violent storm blew his vessel off course. Fergus prayed to Him 'whom the winds and the sea obey' and made a vow that if he was saved, he would acknowledge his survival with some fitting work of piety.

The storm waned and a gentler breeze bore the ship to the coast of Lancashire where Fergus reflected with gratitude on his miraculous deliverance and wondered how to honour his vow. While resting from the ordeal, a voice in a dream instructed him to seek a place named 'Fernyhalgh'. There he would find a crab apple tree bearing fruit without cores, and beneath it a spring of clear water. There he was to build a chapel.

After an exhaustive and unsuccessful search, Fergus eventually reached Preston (originally Priest's Town) where he entered an inn to rest his weary limbs. Some hours later he was disturbed by a milkmaid, the daughter of the landlord. The girl was returning late and in some distress, for she had spent many hours looking for a lost cow which had strayed as far as 'Fernyhalgh'. To his surprise and delight, Fergus noticed that during her search the milkmaid had gathered a small branch from a crab apple tree and the fruit had no core. He immediately extracted a promise from the girl that she would lead him to the place on the following day.

When Fergus reached the spring and found the crab apple tree he knelt and offered a prayer of thanksgiving, for he had found precisely the place described by the voice in his dream. Near the spring he also found a previously undiscovered statue of the Blessed Virgin, and the spring is known to this day as Our Lady's well. According to Martin Gillett, the author of the *Shrines of Our Lady in England and Wales*, there is recorded evidence of the founding of a chapel at Fernyhalgh during the fourteenth century. In 1348 a licence was granted to Thomas Singleton of Broughton for Mass to be offered within the manors of Fernyhalgh, Broughton and Farmunholes for a period of three years. This may explain the origin of the statue of Our Lady which Fergus discovered in or about 1471.

The chapel which Fergus built lay between the present shrine and the M6 motorway. In some accounts the chapel is referred to as a chantry chapel and is mentioned as such in the record of a dispute that took place during the early part of the reign of King Henry VIII.

Fergus's chapel was duly dedicated, under God, to the honour of the Mother of Christ and was known as 'Our Lady's Chapel at Fernyhalgh'. It remained a place of pilgrimage and devotion until 1547 when it was demolished in the reign of Henry VIII's son, King Edward VI. The revenues, the furniture and the bell were all confiscated. According to the Royal Injuctions of that year, all 'wanderings to pilgrimages' were outlawed, as was recitation of the rosary and any form of procession. All chantries and free chapels were assigned to the Crown. In this faraway place, the blow was incomprehensible.

The missionary priest, Christopher Tuttell, takes up the story again, writing some hundred and fifty years after the destruction of the chapel. He describes the demolition of the walls and the removal of foundation stones which were used to build houses nearby. But neighbouring Catholics continued to gather in prayer at Our Lady's well and it became their rendezvous, especially on feast days. For many years, the areas surrounding the vanished chapel continued to be known as Chapel Wood, Chapel Meadow and Chapel House. More than two centuries later, in 1816 there were elderly people who remembered the site and 'the ancient foot-path in the meadow adjoining the walk at the Lady's Well'.

Our Lady's well was never abandoned and in 1685 a new dwelling was built. The ground floor housed the cattle, and upstairs a small chapel was created. The priests who lived here were dressed in local country garb to discourage recognition, and for a while the old way of life returned to Fernyhalgh.

Troubles returned, however, and Christopher Tuttell, now the missionary priest at Our Lady's well, was frequently visited by marauding soldiers who plundered and stripped the chapel. On one occasion, when they came in search of the priest himself, Tuttell hid in a barn for the night when 'the fear of being found out, the severe coldness of the weather, the bustling and squeaking of the mice within, and ye screeching of owles without, disturbed my rest and kept me waking all the time'.

Ladyewell House

Life for Catholics gradually became easier, and in 1723 they began to pray openly at Our Lady's well. Christopher Tuttell was able to end his days at Fernyhalgh in relative peace.

The shrine continued to flourish under a new priest, Anthony Lund, and land was needed to increase the size of the chapel. An area of six acres was purchased a short distance away and work began on a new church. This was to be the church of Our Lady which stands today, and which I had found on my way to Ladyewell.

The somewhat plain and unremarkable exterior of the building is readily explained when one considers the times in which the work was carried out. Many years were to elapse before the passing of the Catholic Emancipation Act in 1829, and Catholic support for the Jacobite rising of 1745 was still fresh in memory. But within the austere walls of the new church at Fernyhalgh an exquisite interior was created, as if in thanksgiving for more peaceful times and in renewed hope for the future.

The stained-glass window depicts the fifteen mysteries of the rosary and statues of St Thomas More and St Edmund Campion remind us of other martyrs who perhaps visited the shrine of Ladyewell. Although there is no written evidence of their visits, the area was blessed with several martyrs who may well have trodden the path to Ladyewell; George Beesley from Goosnargh, Richard Herst from Broughton, John Southworth from Samlesbury, John Wall from Preston, and Father Germanus Helmes, this last being the final priest to die for the faith in England, in 1746.

A particular sadness associated with the opening of the new church in 1794 was the closure of the chapel by the well, when Ladyewell became a school for girls. In 1905 the Sisters of the Holy Child Jesus arrived and a chapel was restored in the house and the statue of Our Lady of Lourdes was placed by the renovated well. For 85 years they tended the spirit of Ladyewell.

In 1987 the shrine at Ladyewell entered a new and remarkable era, with the appointment of Father Benedict Ruscillo and Catherine Stirzaker as custodians of the shrine and of Ladyewell House.

They have assumed responsibility for the welcome and care of the thousands of pilgrims who make their way to Fernyhalgh, and all manner of improvements have been put in train. There are numerous pilgrimages throughout the year and individual visits are welcomed at any time. The shrine is no longer hidden from all but the most determined pilgrims. Instead it is approached by the lane which has been repaired and by gates that stand open in welcome. Inside the house is a small chapel and in the garden, newly laid out paths lead past Our Lady's well to the Martyrs' chapel which

OLD MISSION ALTAR, LADYEWELL

records the names of 300 English martyrs. Until recently the altar of this chapel stood open to the elements, but it is now covered and there is ample bench seating on the lawns for visiting pilgrims.

Beyond this chapel is a Rosary Way, the walls clad in fine blue tiles – a present from friends in Portugal. In a small woodland area, the Stations of the Cross lead through shaded paths and add to the overall atmosphere of prayer.

On the day of my visit I was shown the reliquary on the first floor of the house. It contains wonderful relics and a fascinating array of memorabilia of the Reformation. As chaplain to the shrine, Father Ruscillo shared his prodigious knowledge of penal times and of the relics.

One of the treasures of the reliquary at Ladyewell is a small court cupboard, made by Thomas Burgess in 1560 for the recusant Towneley family of Towneley Hall, outside Burnley. The court cupboard is carved in dark oak and resembles much of the furniture of the period, but in a matter of minutes it can be transformed into an altar, complete with a large drawer in which vestments could be stored. This missionary altar had been made in response to Queen Elizabeth's Act of Uniformity of 1559 which decreed it a grave offence to celebrate Mass or to assist at Mass.

The 'History of the Old Missionary Altar' which is to be found at Ladyewell tells of adventure and bravery as the altar was moved from family to family; it mentions the priests who celebrated Mass at this sacred table, amongst them the martyrs St Edmund Campion, St Edmund Arrowsmith and Blessed John Woodcock.

St Edmund Campion celebrated Mass at this altar in the final months before his arrest in 1581, and the reliquary at Ladyewell contains the vestments he wore on this occasion.

Other relics include those of the twelfth-century martyr St Thomas Becket and of many other holy men and women. With powerful reason, Our Lady's title here at Ladyewell is 'Our Lady of Fernyhalgh, Queen of Martyrs'.

> So, in peaceful memory dwell
> This tranquil spot, this ancient Well,
> And may Our Lady's blessing be,
> Rambling loiterer, e'er with thee.

Shrine – Fernyhalgh

LOCATION/ DIRECTIONS	From M25 Exit J16 M40 M42 North M6 exit J32 Head for Preston/Ribbleton Continue to follow the Ribbleton sign for Haighton – a left at roundabout. Proceed along the Haighton Road for about a quarter of a mile when you will see on your right Fernyhalgh Lane, Ladyewell. Continue along Fernyhalgh Lane until you see St Mary's School and Church. The road continues and then turns right for Ladyewell.
CONTACT TEL. NUMBERS	The Shrine of Our Lady of the Well Ladyewell House Fernyhalgh Lane Fulwood Preston Lancashire Tel. 01772 700181
EMAIL ADDRESS	admin@ladyewell.co.uk
WEB SITE	www.ladyewell.co.uk
SPECIAL DATES/ EVENTS/ FESTIVALS/ PILGRIMAGES	Please contact for diary of events
OPENING TIMES WINTER SUMMER	Ladyewell House 10.00am – 4.00pm Monday to Saturday 11.30am – 2.30pm Sunday 10.00am – 5.00pm Monday to Saturday 11.30am – 2.30pm Sunday

ROSARY GROUP   John Bradburne prayer group which says the
Rosary and Novena prayers every Wednesday at 5pm

ANGLICAN	Christ Church
CHURCH	Victoria Road
AND CONTACT	Fulwood
TEL. NUMBERS	Preston
	Lancs
	Tel. 01772 719210
LOCAL	National Football Museum, Preston!
ATTRACTIONS	
GOOD PUB	Haighton Manor – Restaurant and accommodation, Haighton Green Lane, Preston. Tel. 01772 651432. Approx. 20 minutes walking – a few minutes by car.
PLACES FOR	Bed and Breakfast, evening meal by arrangement
PILGRIMS TO	– Mr. & Mrs. Hardacre, Highlands House,
STAY	D'Urton Lane, Broughton, Preston PR3 5LE. Tel. 01772 861953. A few minutes from Ladyewell by car and approx. 20 minutes walking.

11

Glastonbury

THE LADY CHAPEL
ERECTED ON THE SITE OF
THE ORIGINAL WATTLE CHURCH
AFTER THE GREAT FIRE 1184

GLASTONBURY

South of the Mendip Hills, the Somerset lanes are narrow and in
spring the uncut hedges are threaded with wild campanula and
convolvulus. Orchards and vineyards give way to the first glimpse
of Glastonbury Tor; on its summit is all that remains of the ancient
chapel of St Michael the Archangel.

Beneath his gaze lies the probable birthplace of Christianity in England, and the site of the first Christian church, a place that was for centuries regarded as the English Jerusalem and one of the holiest places on earth. There is a legend that Joseph of Arimathea brought the Christ Child to Glastonbury to tread upon 'England's green and pleasant land' (William Blake: Jerusalem). Another legend claims that Joseph returned to Glastonbury in AD 61. He drove his staff into the ground where it took root and became famous as the Glastonbury Thorn.

It is said that on his second visit, Joseph brought the Holy Grail to England, the Chalice which held the blood of Christ. Generations have believed that the saint buried this treasure here at Glastonbury, and that the spring still flowing at the base of the Tor, its water tainted red with iron, is the place of burial. The air of Glastonbury is filled with such legends; with the sighs of Queen Guinevere as Arthur's funeral barge crosses the waters to Avalon after a lifetime spent in search of the Holy Grail.

There are pagan memories too. The name Glastonbury means 'Isle of Glass', for the land on which the place stands was once surrounded by lake, swamp and woodland. The mound that rose from the water was known as Avalon, meaning 'Isle of Apples'. This was the place to which rich people of pagan times were brought for burial.

Today, the sacred and the profane stalk the streets of Glastonbury, their differences laid bare and accentuated by the dominance of the great abbey ruins, proclaiming that in this place the conflict of light and darkness is a primeval but ever present struggle. The atmosphere is palpably spiritual.

On my arrival in Glastonbury, I find myself standing beside a group of Japanese tourists watching a procession setting off down the street from the square by the old Pilgrim Inn. A Romany caravan, decorated with shooting stars and signs of the zodiac, is drawn by a grey pony and driven by a man who is bald apart from his long grey pigtail. His companions are New Age travellers with Mohican haircuts, clad in black with metal-studded boots: two women in billowing gypsy skirts run laughing beside them. A small dog circles around this strange group, barking ecstatically.

Within the town there is an air of the occult; alleyways lead to courtyards signposted with promises of spells and cures for all. In one shop, full of crystals and figures of witches and gnomes, I commiserate with the owner at the ear-splitting screech that fills the air. He tells me that it is an eastern mantra. The followers of strange cults walk the streets, whey-faced and sad; despair hangs

GLASTONBURY

heavy in the air. St Michael the Archangel seems an inspired choice as guardian of the holy places of Glastonbury and judge of such goings-on.

Under his watchful eye are the remains of the magnificent abbey that is even older than Westminster. I walk through the entrance and in the evening light the shadows seem barely to conceal the ghosts of kings and queens, saints and sinners and the vast multitude of pilgrims who once walked here. The birds are ending their evening song and as I pass over the newly-mown grass, through the remains of ancient halls and cloisters, I have to shake myself to realize that the only sound to be heard now is the gentle click of the beads in my hand.

I cross the lawns to the remains of the Romanesque chapel of Our Lady; the great stone archway with carved figures of the saints weathered by the ravages of time, the symmetry of the vaulted ceiling interrupted by vacant skies. After the Abbot's kitchen, this is the most perfectly preserved area in the precincts of the ruined abbey.

Dunstan

On this spot the first Christian church in England was apparently built. According to legend, the Holy Child blessed the little chapel in honour of his mother when Joseph of Arimathea brought him to England. In another account it was built soon after the Council of Ephesus in 431 had declared Our Lady to be the one who gave birth to God, the *Theotokos*, to confound those who were arguing about the nature of her motherhood. The building of this chapel began the long allegiance of England to Mary which was so much a part of the English character and caused England to be considered as the dower of Mary.

During the centuries that followed, the new abbey rose up around the small church and the cemetery nearby. When the Saxon King Ina arrived in 725, he declared that the little wattle church was the *Ecclesia Vetusta Beatissimae Virginis* (the old church of the most blessed Virgin), the foremost church in Britain, and the beginning of all Christian religion in this country.

The invasion of the Danes nearly brought the entire enterprise to its knees but for the intervention of a man of Glastonbury who emerged from a life of prayer in a hermit's cell in 943. He insisted on the full observance of the Benedictine Rule, and Glastonbury became famous for its learning. By the time of his death, St Dunstan had not only revived this monastery but had restored the monasteries of England to such an extent that Glastonbury was considered the mother house of them all.

But such glories were not to last. In 1184 Dunstan's fine monastery burnt to the ground, and with it the Lady chapel, although the ancient statue of the Blessed Virgin from the old wattle church survived.

With astonishing speed a new monastery rose from the ashes and the first part to be completed was the magnificent Lady chapel. The new abbey church was named in honour of SS Peter and Paul, and the abbey buildings with the monastery itself were once more dedicated to the Blessed Virgin Mary.

While digging near Our Lady's chapel in the year 1190 monks unearthed what they believed to be the remains of King Arthur and his wife Guinevere. During the thirteenth century, King Edward I and his wife, Eleanor of Castille, arrived at Glastonbury in Holy Week and witnessed the reburial of the legendary king and his bride whose hair was said to be 'delicately braided'. A small plaque by the remains of the high altar marks the place of burial.

As soon as the new building was complete, the pilgrims returned. All summer long, the lanes of Somerset thronged with crowds, especially on Our Lady's birthday, 8 September, when festivities were prolonged. The gifts that were brought to the shrine on such occasions were often recorded.

During the sixth century St David came from Wales and left a great sapphire which was a cause of wonder for a thousand years. In the fourteenth century, Queen Philippa, wife of Edward III, left a silver rosary with gold paternoster beads for Our Lady, and there were always bunches of wild flowers, gathered from the hedgerows, that were brought by the poorer pilgrims.

This was the age of 'Merrie England'; pilgrimage was part of the English way of life when rich and poor, famous and the infamous, journeyed together to visit the shrines of the Virgin Mary and of the numerous saints whom they considered to be their friends; these were friends whose help and advice they enlisted in the turbulent events of their daily lives.

It was not to last. In 1535 Thomas Cromwell's emissary, Dr Layton, visited Glastonbury in search of evidence to justify closure of the abbey; none could be found. It hardly mattered, for the abbot had been prejudged, and the verdict was revealed in the remembrance of Cromwell, the Lord Privy Seal – 'item: the Abbot of Glastonbury to be tried at Glaston and also executyd there with his complyeys'. The abbot and two of his monks were dragged through Glastonbury on hurdles and hanged on the Tor on 15 November 1539.

The abbey was dismantled, the numerous buildings razed to the ground, but the survival of much of the Lady chapel suggests that there was a reluctance to complete the destruction. Perhaps a lingering gratitude to Our Lady of Glastonbury held back the hand of the spoilers. To the right of the south doorway of the Lady chapel the well-known 'Jesus' stone, carved by some devout monk as he finished his twelfth-century labours, remained untouched. It is there to this day.

Rebirth

The shadows were lengthening and the birds were silent. Overcome by the pity of it all, the desecration of magnificent buildings built to the honour of God, the destruction of priceless manuscripts and treasures which were part of the history of England, all lost and destroyed at the whim of one man's greed – I turned my steps towards home.

As I looked back across the empty lawns, at the soaring arches of the abbey church, fringed with grass against the moonlight, I felt that throngs of monks and pilgrims to Glastonbury over the centuries were taking up their prayer in the peace of the night.

The following day, the sun was shining and the shadows had

dispersed. Even the New Age travellers were smiling as they loped along the streets – their dogs with noses in the air, as they went together in search of food; and I went in search of the new shrine of Our Lady of Glastonbury.

Leaving the Market Cross in the middle of the town, I walked along Magdalene Street to the lane lined with the sixteenth-century almshouses of St Patrick which leads to the entrance to the abbey. For four hundred years, the ruins of this holy place in Christendom lay silent and abandoned. But even in the darkest days of persecution recusant Catholics would still come to pray at the remains of Our Lady's shrine.

At the beginning of the twentieth century the land passed into the hands of trustees acting on behalf of the Anglican church. Under their guidance archaeologists and researchers turned their attention to what was left of the once-great abbey, and gradually the ruins were laid bare and skilfully restored. The small museum which opened recently gives a detailed and graphic impression of the early life of the monastery and is well worth a visit.

I walked on, past the shops now opening; the sound of tinkling glass and pan pipes mingled with the smell of herbal teas wafting from doorways. Further down Magdalene Street I came to the Catholic church and the shrine of Our Lady standing opposite the abbey ruins on land that was once part of the abbot's park of Wirral. The name is taken from 'weary-all', so named by the first missionaries after their lengthy and exhausting journey.

The shrine of the Blessed Virgin had never been forgotten, and in 1920 a small Catholic church was built in Glastonbury. Pilgrimages began again under the inspiration of the Guild of Our Lady of Ransom. Before long the congregation and visitors had outgrown the small church and in 1941 a new church in honour of Our Lady of Glastonbury was consecrated by Bishop Lee of Clifton, in whose diocese Glastonbury stands.

All that is known of the original shrine statue is that it disappeared, either to be burned or to be sold abroad. When the time came to replace the figure in a new shrine, the carved statue was based on the seal of John Chinnock who had been Abbot of Glastonbury at the end of the fourteenth century. The sculptor Philip Lindsey Clarke undertook the commission. His work can also be seen in Kent at the shrine of Our Lady in Aylesford.

In 1955 the new statue was blessed by the Apostolic Delegate, Archbishop O'Hara, before a gathering of 18,000 pilgrims and the shrine was officially restored in the name of the Holy See. Ten years later a new Apostolic Delegate crowned the statue with gold

GLASTONBURY

given by the parishioners in the presence of another vast crowd.

In the same year a tapestry was commissioned to hang above the altar. The artist, a Benedictine monk of Prinknash Abbey, Louis Barlow, has recorded the history of the shrine in two parts, to hang on either side of the statue of the Blessed Virgin. The Benedictine connection with Our Lady's shrine is thus maintained, and the titular abbot of Glastonbury is once more a Benedictine monk from nearby Downside Abbey.

Glastonbury is the foundation stone of the Dowry of Mary, and in this new springtime of shared Christian devotion, the old English custom of pilgrimage to Glastonbury is once more a vibrant reality. There are frequent pilgrimages by many different groups, which have included Youth Two Thousand whose young members come to Glastonbury on prayer weekends and retreats. In the summer there are two days of processions on the second weekend in July undertaken by Anglicans and Catholics. On the Sunday, the statue of Our Lady of Glastonbury is carried from her new shrine to the summit of the Tor. Prayers are offered in Tor Field and the procession then passes through the town to the ruins of the abbey where Mass is celebrated.

Before I leave this ancient place, I return to stand before the statue of Our Lady of Glastonbury. She stands serenely gazing down, her body slightly leaning as she holds her Son in her left arm and in her right hand a flowering bush, perhaps the Glastonbury thorn. As a reminder of the ancient wattle chapel, she stands in front of a wattle hurdle.

Beneath the figure is a copy of the words engraved next to the Lady chapel in the Abbey ruins, JESUS MARIA. When the upheavals of history fade, these are the words that remain.

Shrine – Glastonbury

LOCATION/ DIRECTIONS	From M25, exit J15 M4 West, exit J15 M5 South, exit J23 A39 to Glastonbury The Church is situated opposite Glastonbury Abbey on Magdalene Street
CONTACT TEL. NUMBERS	Church of Our Lady St Mary St Mary's Presbytery Magdalene Street Glastonbury Somerset BA6 9EJ Tel. 01458 832203
WEB SITE	www.glastonburyshrine.co.uk
TIMES OF SERVICES	MASS Saturday 6.00pm Sunday 8.30am and 10.30am Monday to Saturday 10.00am Holy Days 10.00am and 7.00pm Latin (1962) 12.15pm 3rd Sunday of each month
SPECIAL DATES/ EVENTS/FESTIVALS PILGRIMAGES	Glastonbury Pilgrimage – 2nd Sunday in July www.glastonburyabbey.com Tel. 01458 443732
ANGLICAN CHURCH AND CONTACT TEL. NUMBERS	St Johns and St Benedict Benedict Street Glastonbury Tel. 01458 832362
LOCAL ATTRACTIONS	Glastonbury Abbey, Open Daily www.glastonburyabbey.com Glastonbury Festival – Last Weekend in June www.glastonbury.co.uk Glastonbury Tor (National Trust Monument) Chalice Well Gardens www.chalicewell.org.uk Wells Cathedral Somerset Rural Life Museum, Glastonbury

GOOD PUBS	Numerous pubs in town centre
PLACES FOR PILGRIMS TO STAY	Glastonbury Tourist Information 9 High Street Glastonbury Tel. 01458 832954 Email: glastonbury.tic@ukonline.co.uk

12

Hartley

HARTLEY

The journey to this unusual shrine leads into the heart of Kent, the area once known as the Garden of England. Kent has long been an area of orchards and hop fields although in recent years the farmers have lost out to overseas competition. Roads and country lanes take us through fields of grazing sheep, oast houses and orchards of apples and cherries. To the north, the ancient Pilgrims' Way runs from Canterbury to Winchester, and the many Saxon churches in the area are a reminder that Kent was once mission territory. It was here that St Augustine of Canterbury arrived in the year 597 with instructions from Pope St Gregory to refound the Church in England.

There have been Christians in this area since the days of the Romans and the ancient parish church of All Saints in Hartley has served their needs since Saxon times. Before the Reformation a chantry chapel also stood in Hartley, but this was swept away in the sixteenth century. At the beginning of the twentieth century Catholic worship was at last restored.

Leaving the M25 motorway to the north, the route passes briefly through deep countryside before reaching the ribbon development between Hartley and New Ash Green where a large thatched barn looms into view, a small cross beside the immense roof.

Beside the barn with its large sign announcing 'St Francis de Sales Catholic Church' the lane leads past a car park that was once an orchard, to houses that were built by the founder of this oratory, as it was then known, and the shrine. Inside the church the first impression is of a stable beneath the beams and of the underside of the thatched roof. Mice were running along a beam above and small seeds fell to the ground. This beautiful barn is reminiscent of the stable at Bethlehem, and nothing could be more fitting as the setting for the shrine of Our Lady of Hartley.

The shrine statue stands facing the entrance to the newly-built extension of the barn. The figure of Mary is crowned and royally clad in richly decorated robes with the Holy Child on her left arm. A clue to the origin of the statue may be found in the early shrine to Our Lady of Montaigu which lies near Louvain in the archdiocese of Malines-Brussels.

Many centuries ago a huge and solitary oak stood here on a steep mound rising from the surrounding lowlands, a beacon that could be seen for miles around and which marked a long abandoned place of Druid worship. In the fourteenth century a figure of Our Lady was placed in a niche on the tree.

The statue of Our Lady of Hartley is known to be Belgian and of the late eighteenth century. It bears a remarkable similarity to a statue of Our Lady that stands in the town of Lierre, between Malines and Antwerp; it is known that in 1605 the Sheriff of Lierre visited a famous oak tree shrine at Montaigu and was given a piece of the tree from which the statue at Lierre was carved.

Although the statue of Our Lady of Hartley is more natural in appearance than the statue at Lierre this may be attributed to the later date of the carving and does not necessarily rule out an intention to copy the statue at Montaigu.

It is not, however, known precisely where or when the Hartley statue was carved. We know that it dates from the late eighteenth century, and we can also be sure that the rose and shamrock robes were designed and sewn by Anglo-Irish Dominican nuns who were exiled in Belgium, having fled from France following the French Revolution.

The reason for the choice of the English rose and the Irish shamrock for Our Lady's robes may seem obvious in view of the connections of the nuns with both England and Ireland. But there may be more to this than meets the eye. A number of English recusant Catholics found their way to the Low Countries after the Reformation and, during the seventeenth century, Catholic soldiers from England and Ireland were amongst those who enlisted in the religious wars of the Netherlands. There is a record of the Jesuit Walter Talbot leading Irish mercenaries on pilgrimage before going into battle. Did these young soldiers also come to pray for protection before the statue which we know as Our Lady of Hartley? If so, the nuns would have been aware that the English rose and the Irish shamrock would be poignant reminders of home for these men.

The Barn Oratory

The terrors and flights of the French Revolution may well have caused the Hartley statue to be lost to Belgium and resulted in its eventual arrival in a second-hand shop in London. Here it fell under the gaze of a remarkable woman, Miss Beatrice Davies-Cook, as she walked along Church Street in Kensington in 1913.

Miss Davies-Cooke was searching for just such a figure for the church she was endowing in the Kent village of Hartley. Beatrice Davies-Cook had recently become a Catholic and had decided to mark her conversion by providing a suitable place of worship in an area which needed a church. In 1910, the parish priest of Northfleet, which included the outlying area of Hartley, had started to urge his parishioners to pray for a solution to the problem of a far-flung parish with no suitable place of worship in the Hartley area. Two years later their prayers were answered. Miss Davies-Cook learnt of their needs and bought Middle Farm with the intention of creating an oratory where Mass would be celebrated and a new parish might one day be established.

Miss Davies-Cook's purchase stood in ninety-four acres of fertile land. At the beginning of the last century the area around Hartley was a world away from the busy surburban sprawl which encroaches upon it today. The apple and cherry orchards, the hop fields and the wooded hedgerows created a haven of blossom and wild flowers. In the early autumn, families living in the East End of London flocked to the area to spend a holiday hop-picking.

When Beatrice Davies-Cook first arrived at Hartley, the great tithe barn was full of mangel-wurzels which were swiftly cleared. Once the floor had been levelled and concreted, the enormous door under the porch was sealed off and made into the arch of the shrine in which the newly acquired statue of the Blessed Virgin was to stand. The first service was held in the church in 1913 on the feast of St Joseph, 19 March. When a mission was preached in the following September, there were ninety people present.

Furnishings were gradually gathered together for oratory and shrine. Some were exotic; one set of vestments is said to have come from the last Emperor of China.

Over the years, the magnificent building with its huge thatched roof has proved a mixed blessing, and there was even a time when the building of a new church was considered. The thatch is made with 'long straw' rather than Norfolk reed; long straw is difficult to obtain and has a shorter lifespan than reed.

It is a highly skilled task to rethatch such a large area and, when this could finally be undertaken, six layers of thatch had first to be removed which resulted in the old thatch on the south side slithering to the ground and momentarily burying the two thatchers. The tarpaulins used to cover the gaping hole that was left were torn off by storms and gales which soaked the church furnishings beneath.

Work on the roof was carried out by John Kenward, whose family had been Kent thatchers for six generations. While working on the new thatch, John found his father's old snuff boxes hidden in the roof. Fortunately the repaired roof and the sympathetic extension to the barn have ensured the preservation of the church, and English Heritage is now keenly interested in the building. The newly-acquired series of jewel-like stained-glass windows by Paul Quail cast an incandescent light into the shadows beneath the beams.

Sunday Mass has been celebrated at the church without a break since 1913. During the First World War Miss Davies-Cooke invited refugees from Belgium, Austria and Hungary to join the congregation, and later some German prisoners of war came to join them. Soldiers were once again praying before Our Lady's statue. This multinational congregation created a renewed interest in the oratory and resulted in the shrine at Hartley becoming part of the chain of Marian shrines inaugurated during the Great War.

It was not until 1921 that official permission was granted for the establishment of the shrine at Hartley, when a friend of Miss Davies-Cook mentioned the shrine at Hartley to Pope Benedict XV. The Holy Father granted the necessary permission and gave his blessing to the rosary that is now held by the Virgin.

For the first twenty-four years of its existence, priests came down from London each week to celebrate Mass at the oratory, as it was then known, usually making the journey by motorbike. In 1937 the parish and shrine became the responsibility of the Carmelite Fathers. Seventeen years later, in 1954, over four thousand people came on pilgrimage to the oratory during the Marian year.

In 1980 Hartley acquired its own priest, and the Carmelites no longer travelled over from Aylesford. The area has grown beyond recognition and now boasts a flourishing primary school. The barn, however, remains as a reminder of more rural days and the triumph of one woman's faith.

Shrine – Hartley

LOCATION/ DIRECTIONS	From M25 Exit J2 A2 A227 to Meopham B2360 towards Longfield, follow signs to Hartley Church Road is on the corner of Stack Lane
CONTACT TEL. NUMBERS	Our Lady of Hartley St Francis de Sales Church Road Hartley Dartford Kent DA3 8DW Tel. 01474 705361
TIMES OF SERVICES	MASS Saturday (for Sunday) 5.30pm Sunday 8.30am, 10.30am, 6.30pm Monday to Thursday 9.15am Friday 7.45pm (followed by adoration 1st Fridays) Saturday 9.15am (followed by Rosary), (in Latin on 1st Sat.)
SPECIAL DATES/ EVENTS/ FESTIVALS/ PILGRIMAGES	Pilgrimage groups who wish to arrange for Mass to be said or would like to use the tea rooms etc., please make prior arrangements
ANGLICAN CHURCH AND CONTACT TEL. NUMBERS	All Saints Church The Rectory 3 St John's Lane Hartley Kent DA3 8ET Tel. 01474 703819
LOCAL ATTRACTIONS	Brands Hatch Racing Circuit, Fawkham, Longfield Bluewater Shopping Centre (largest in Europe!) J2 M25

GOOD PUBS	There are several pubs around the area and in the village
PLACES FOR PILGRIMS TO STAY	Tourist Information Centre Tel. 01474 337600 email: info@towncentric.co.uk

13

Ipswich

When the Danish invaders first reached the east coast of England in the ninth century, they recognized in the extraordinary atmosphere of the area some unearthly quality which caused them to refer to 'selig Suffolk' – holy Suffolk. In later centuries, the wealth of the Suffolk wool traders encouraged the building of numerous churches, many of which remain. There is a saying that, wherever the traveller finds himself in Suffolk, there is always a church in view.

Suffolk churches are renowned for their airy beauty; it is perhaps the very destruction of their stained-glass windows by the Reformers that fills their ancient naves and chancels with the extraordinary Suffolk light, frequently beneath the gaze of delicately-carved angels.

Sometimes referred to as the largest village in Suffolk, Ipswich has two distinct personalities. It is a successful industrial town with a population of some 150,000 people and a famous football team. There are, at the same time, unmistakable reminders of the past: of a time when streets now clogged with traffic were thronged with pilgrims from all over England making their way to the shrine of Our Lady of Grace.

Before the Dissolution there were thirty-nine churches in the town and four religious foundations. The most renowned was the shrine and chapel of Our Lady of Grace of Ipswich, famous for two and a half centuries throughout the Christian world, and ranking second in England only to her sister shrine at Walsingham.

There are twelve medieval churches still standing, not all of them in use and some in a better state of preservation than others. Five of today's parish churches are dedicated to the Blessed Virgin; they bear witness to a tradition of Marian devotion that has existed here since the twelfth century. Although nothing remains today of the ancient chapel of Our Lady of Grace, the revival of the shrine has taken place in a manner that seems almost miraculous.

A small byway in the town centre, Lady Lane, marks the spot where the chapel of Our Lady of Grace once stood. The lane is well hidden and leads from Wolsey car park through streets of half-timbered houses that were once the homes of the wealthy wool merchants and are now shops and offices.

A bronze wall statue of Our Lady of Grace marks the site of the shrine, and a small plaque beneath explains the wonder of the shrine that once stood in this place.

In the hurly-burly atmosphere of a prosperous industrial town, it is hard to imagine a time when visitors came here principally to meet others of like mind and to pray at Our Lady's shrine. The town was renowned as the home of the shrine, and for the importance of its situation on the pilgrim route to Walsingham.

The long journey to Walsingham through the glorious East Anglian countryside would have been punctuated with stops at the shrines of Clare, Sudbury and above all, at Ipswich.

Early records list proudly the rich and famous who passed through the town. In 1297 King Edward I chose to bring his daughter Princess Elizabeth to Ipswich for her marriage to John, Count of Holland, in the chapel of Our Lady of Grace. Catherine of Aragon, having visited the shrine once, was reported in the borough archives to have risen with the lark, as it appears she paid another visit to the Lady chapel as early as six o'clock. In 1522 her husband, King Henry VIII, attended Mass at Our Lady's shrine. St Thomas More came several times to Ipswich and wrote a detailed account of the visit of one of his friends, Sir Roger Wentworth, whose daughter had been cured of an illness after visiting Our Lady of Grace.

The great Cardinal Wolsey was born in Ipswich in 1472, the son of a local butcher. At the height of his meteoric career, Wolsey kept a household of one thousand people and was said to travel with silver pillars and pole-axes carried before him. Wolsey's grasp of diplomacy prompted the Venetian ambassador, Sebastian Giustiniani, to remark: 'He alone transacts the same business which occupies all the magistrates, offices and councils of Venice.'

Wolsey founded schools and colleges of unparalleled splendour and amongst these a great college in Ipswich in addition to his College of Christ Church at Oxford. Having swept away several monasteries in East Anglia, including the Augustinian priory on whose site he wished to place his college at Ipswich, the money was raised for the foundation and building commenced.

The Cardinal intended that the chapel of Our Lady of Grace should be united with his great venture. He ordered a yearly pilgrimage to the shrine to take place on the feast of the Birthday of the Blessed Virgin, 8 September.

The enterprise was short-lived and there had been time for only one of his pilgrimages to the shrine before the King's favour evaporated. Wolsey's attempts to arrange a royal annulment from Queen Catherine of Aragon had come to nothing. He fell from grace in 1529, and his college was destroyed almost as soon as the building had been completed.

At the time of the Dissolution, Henry's chief minister, Thomas Cromwell, appointed Sir Thomas Rushe, Sheriff of Norfolk, as Visitor to 'report' on the shrine of our Lady of Grace of Ipswich. The result was inevitable; in 1538 the shrine was closed and the contents removed to London, there to be destroyed and burnt.

But were they? There is no doubt that the majority of the statues from Our Lady's shrine were burnt at Chelsea but there is evidence to suggest that some of these holy objects escaped such a fate. Many of the priceless statues and relics which had been looted in haste were sold into Europe to fill the King's coffers; an expensive war with Catholic Europe was becoming a distinct and expensive possibility. Some few pious objects and statues that were neither burnt nor sold found their way into safe keeping to emerge unscathed in more peaceful times. It is believed that the statue of Our Lady of Grace of Ipswich was among these.

Nettuno

Far away, on the west coast of Italy lies the small town of Nettuno where in 1969 Pope Paul VI opened the *Santuario di Nostra Signora delle Grazie e di Santa Maria Goretti,* the sanctuary of Our Lady of Grace and the twentieth-century Italian martyr Maria Goretti. In the alcove above the altar is a statue which is known locally as 'The English Lady': the people of Nettuno believe firmly that the statue came originally from Ipswich.

The story goes back to the Jubilee Year of 1550 in Italy, when Our Lady, 'loathing to remain in that profane climate' of England, apparently let it be known that she wished to be honoured in the small town of Nettuno.

Little is known of the statue's apparent rescue from the place in Chelsea where the bonfires awaited. It is, however, only too easy to imagine the opportunities for escape offered by ships berthed in the Thames nearby and bound for Italy, their holds filled with merchandise. Rising fog from the river would have provided ample cover for sailors making for the shore to remove the statue of Our Lady of Grace from beneath the noses of Cromwell's men. A swift return to the waiting boat would have been essential, and a silent row across the water to the ship which was ready to slip anchor and set sail for the open sea. The several accounts of the events which followed differ only in detail.

The rescue vessel was apparently a large galleon of Spanish design, with a lofty stern to enable the ship to race before a temperate wind. But it was not built for stormy seas, and this weakness was exposed in the violent storm that raged off the coast of Nettuno for three days in 1550. From the shore it was apparent that no ship, however well built, could survive the towering waves. Fearing that his ship was about to be wrecked, the captain made for the lagoon off the shores of Nettuno, and prayers were offered to the Blessed Virgin imploring her protection. The waves subsided and calm was restored.

The following day, impatient to be on his way, the captain gave orders to set sail once more, and the prow of the galleon turned out to sea. Almost immediately the crew found themselves struggling with the rigging as the storm returned in force to batter the ship. Renewing their prayers, the vessel limped back into Nettuno. It was at last understood that this was the place where Our Lady wished to remain and the statue was taken ashore.

It seems to be the stuff of legend, but the story is intriguingly confirmed in archives both civil and ecclesiastic. It is also mentioned in guide books and histories of the town.

Few details are available concerning the exact appearance of the statue that stood in the chapel in Ipswich before the Dissolution, but such information as there is indicates remarkable similarities between Our Lady of Grace of Ipswich and the statue in Nettuno. During restoration in 1959, the words IU? ARET GRATIOSUS, Thou art gracious, were found engraved beneath the base of the statue. Scholarly research has identified the legend as medieval English. In 1938 the statue had been positively identified as Our Lady of Grace of Ipswich by Martin Gillett of the Ecumenical Society of the Blessed Virgin Mary, the leading authority on the shrines of Our Lady in England and Wales.

During the years leading up to the Second World War, the figure was in the care of the Passionist Fathers who placed it in the sanctuary of Our Lady of Grace and St Maria Goretti in the St Roch district of the town. It was placed standing on a ship as a reminder

OUR LADY OF GRACE

of the great adventure of its arrival. Today the statue stands unadorned, no longer aboard ship, and marked by the scars of the 1944 Allied landings which took place at Nettuno and Anzio.

In 1975 the first pilgrimage took place from Ipswich to Nettuno, led by the late Stanley Smith, whose book *The Madonna of Ipswich* resulted from his researches into the shrine of Our Lady of Grace.

ST. MARY ELMS, IPSWICH

This happy occasion was marked with the gift of silver plaques presented by the people of Ipswich to the town of Nettuno, and the pilgrimage has been repeated. In 2003 a group made up of several denominations set off on pilgrimage once more from Ipswich, and was received with great warmth as the pilgrimage reached Nettuno.

Some twenty years ago, the Guild of Our Lady of Ipswich was revived and later became known as the Meryem Ana Foundation, after the Holy House of Mary at Ephesus which had been shown in a dream to the nineteenth-century German visionary Anna Katharina Emmerick. Anna Katharina had seen Meryem Ana as a place where the great faiths of Islam and Christianity coexisted peacefully. The name of the Guild of Our Lady of Ipswich was changed to Meryem Ana, in accordance with the wish of many Anglicans and Catholics, to acknowledge their combined efforts to restore pilgrimage and devotion to the shrine of Our Lady of Grace.

At the beginning of the new millennium, the restoration of the shrine has at last become a reality, the culmination of many years of prayer. A copy of the original statue of Our Lady of Grace based on the statue at Nettuno has been carved from English oak by the sculptor Robert Mellamphy. It is installed in Ipswich in the beautiful Anglo-Catholic church of St Mary at the Elms. This remarkable building is easily recognized by its landmark red tower and outstanding Norman doorway. The statue of Our Lady of Grace joins an earlier statue of Our Lady of Walsingham already in the church. This is truly an ecumenical shrine that must indeed be the gift of Our Lady of Grace of Ipswich.

Every year a pilgrimage takes place on the Sunday nearest to 8 September, the feast of Our Lady's Birthday, which brings together Anglicans and Catholics. The first pilgrimage took place in 1978, 450 years to the day after the pilgrimage ordered by Cardinal Wolsey on 8 September 1528.

The pilgrimage now begins at St Peter's Anglican church which stands beside the ancient arch of the courtyard gateway, all that remains of the Cardinal's great college. From St Peter's, the pilgrims make their way through the town to the site of the original shrine in Lady Lane. In a remarkable way this ecumenical pilgrimage brings to a close nearly four hundred years of strife and dissension and gives great cause for hope.

Shrine – Ipswich

LOCATION/ DIRECTIONS	From the M25, exit J28 Take A12 to Colchester/Ipswich Follow signs to city centre Park at 'Civic Centre' or 'Wolsey' Car Parks Walk down Black Horse Lane into Elm Street BY TRAIN London Liverpool Street reaches Ipswich in just over 1 hour MEMORIAL STATUE AND PLAQUE The original site of the shrine can be found in Lady Lane (look high for the street name!), opposite the pedestrian crossing from 'Wolsey' Car Park
CONTACT TEL. NUMBERS	St Mary at the Elms The Vicarage 68 Black Horse Lane Ipswich Tel. 01473 216484
WEB SITE	www.stmaryattheelms.org.uk
TIMES OF SERVICES	Sunday 10.45am Monday 12.30pm Tuesday 1.10pm Wednesday 10.00am, and 12 noon to 2.00pm Time of Tranquillity Thursday 12.30pm Friday 12.30pm Saturday 10.00am
SPECIAL DATES/ EVENTS/ FESTIVALS/ PILGRIMAGES	2nd Sunday in September, pilgrimage walk through the town of Ipswich from St Peter's to Lady Lane
ROMAN CATHOLIC CHURCH AND CONTACT TEL. NUMBERS	St Pancras 1 Orwell Place Ipswich IP4 1BD Tel. 01473 252596 Email: stpancras.Parishpriest@btinternet.com

LOCAL ATTRACTIONS	St Peter's Church, adjacent to Wolsey's Gateway, an interior courtyard gateway, all that remains of the school planned by Cardinal Wolsey Christchurch Mansion was the site of the Augustinian Priory of the Holy Trinity; museum and gallery including Constable and Gainsborough paintings Ipswich Historic Churches Trail (contact Tourist Information 01473 258070)
GOOD PUBS	Black Horse, Black Horse Lane, behind St Mary's Contact Tourist Information www.ipswich.gov.uk
PLACES FOR PILGRIMS TO STAY	Contact St Mary at the Elms, who can help with hospitality for pilgrims

CHAPEL OF
OUR LADY
OF THE
MOUNT
485

14

King's Lynn

Until the Reformation this little harbour town in West Norfolk was known as Lynn Episcopi, Bishop's Lynn and despite its renaming under Henry VIII it is known locally simply as 'Lynn'.

The little round chapel that was once the chapel of Our Lady of the Mount reminds one of the nursery rhyme about 'the king of the castle' – so slight a fortress appears to be sitting on a very small round hill. On the day of our visit we followed a map drawn for us by the parish priest of the church of Our Lady of the Annunciation. This led us through the heavy traffic on London Road and along a peaceful avenue beneath a canopy of trees and across the park, weaving past some children playing football, to Red Mount Chapel, as it is known locally. The upper floor was clad in scaffolding, and the little building seemed beleaguered on the summit of its small mound. Beyond the park lie the muddy waters of the Great Ouse River, the remains of the Wash as it rushes over Bull Dog Sand and into this estuary.

On the east side of the river there was once a chapel dedicated to the Blessed Virgin. It stood beside the bridge over which pilgrims crossed to reach the lane leading to the chapel of Our Lady of the Mount. This was a stopping place for pilgrims travelling to England's Nazareth at Walsingham, twenty-five miles to the east. Some came by sea from the Continent, others by land from the north of England, and the ferry that plied its way across the river still operates today.

In 1879 the antiquary Edmund Waterton wrote of the chapel: 'Many offerings were made to the image of our Ladye, in her chapel on the Mount of Lynn, by pilgrims who visited it on their way to Walsingham.' There may have been an earlier shrine on this little mound, for it was already known as Ladye Hill when building began in 1485: Waterton certainly mentions the founding of Our Lady's Guild at Lynn in 1329.

The chapel of Our Lady of the Mount is an extaordinary build-ing, some 17 ft long and 14 ft wide, making the shape of a cross that is held in an octagonal surround.

Even in the fifteenth century, crowd control had to be consid-ered. In order to reach the top chapel with its delicate fan-vaulted ceiling, a double staircase was installed which enabled visitors to enter by one door and leave by another.

In the centuries following the Dissolution, the Catholic popula-tion melted away from Lynn. The little chapel on the hill was no longer visited by pilgrims, who were then cared for spiritually by recusant households such as Oxborough and others nearby. By 1823 the building had become a stable for horses, a cause of heart-felt concern to one local inhabitant who managed to restore this architectural gem.

For many years a custodian was available to admit visitors, but the chapel is now in the hands of King's Lynn council and firmly closed. The building is, however, being repaired, although the shrine itself is still to be restored.

The Catholic Emancipation Act of 1829 opened the way to a restoration of Catholic presence in Lynn and a new church was designed by A. W. Pugin and completed in 1845. This rapidly deteriorated, and the parish priest, Father George Wrigglesworth, received many complaints about the lack of comfort; even Catholic guests of the Royal Family at nearby Sandringham voiced their objection.

For many years Father Wrigglesworth had longed to restore the long-abandoned shrine of Our Lady of Walsingham twenty-five miles distant, which had lacked any Catholic presence since the Reformation. He proposed to ask Pope Leo XIII if he could re-establish the shrine of Our Lady of Walsingham at King's Lynn and, together with the co-founder of the Guild of Our Lady of Ransom, Father Philip Fletcher, he set off to Rome. The Holy Father agreed to their plans for a shrine in honour of Our Lady of Walsingham and signed the necessary document in February 1897.

In June of the same year a new and more comfortable Catholic church was opened in the town. It had been designed by a local architect, Mr W. Lunn, and was dedicated to Our Lady of the Annunciation.

The shrine chapel is attached to the church, and is a perfect small-scale reproduction of the Holy House of Loreto – itself a replica of the Holy House of Nazareth. The figure of Our Lady was made in the Austrian village of Oberammergau and was based on the copy of a picture from the church that had once been the titular possession of the sixteenth-century English cardinal, Reginald Pole. The statue now stands above a small altar, beneath a wooden ceiling painted a deep blue and strewn with stars, above the walls strangely constructed in waving lines of brick. The figure of Our Lady arrived at King's Lynn on 19 August 1897, to be greeted at the station by crowds not only of Lynn but from all parts of England. The road from the station was lined with people, and after a pause at the pre-Reformation chapel of Our Lady of the Mount to recite the Salve Regina, the statue was received into the shrine chapel of the Church of the Annunciation. The following day the first pilgrimage to Walsingham since the Reformation took place, covering some twenty-five miles. The original poster announcing this event still hangs in the sacristy: an historic document, slightly brown with age.

While these momentous events were taking place at Lynn, Walsingham itself was awakening from its long sleep. Miss Charlotte Boyd was busily occupied in restoring the ancient Slipper Chapel outside the village of Little Walsingham, and at the same time endeavouring to interest the Catholic hierarchy in the possibility of restoring the ancient shrine of Our Lady of Walsingham in this little chapel, close to the home of the pre-Reformation shrine at Walsingham Priory.

The years passed by, and the Guild of Our Lady of Ransom continued to lead annual pilgrimages from the shrine of Our Lady of Walsingham at King's Lynn to the village of Walsingham. It was not until 1934 that Miss Boyd's dream at last became a reality. She herself was long dead, but in that year the national shrine of Our Lady of Walsingham was established once more at the Slipper Chapel outside Little Walsingham, and Lynn relinquished its claim.

The King's Lynn shrine has not been overwhelmed by the proximity of its sister shrine at Walsingham; it is a place of pilgrimage throughout the summer, continuing the tradition that began in the fifteenth-century chapel of Our Lady of the Mount barely half a mile from the restored shrine.

The purpose of the unique little chapel on the hill is now a forlorn memory in the public mind, and yet the sign by the ancient door that announces the 'Chapel of Our Lady of the Mount 1485' hangs above an old water stoup on the wall and shows little sign of fading. Perhaps it is waiting for the day when its doors will open once more to welcome pilgrims content to rest here and say a prayer.

Shrine – King's Lynn

LOCATION/ DIRECTIONS	From M25, exit J27 M11, exit J14 to the A14 Follow A10 to King's Lynn At junction with A47 follow Town Centre signs and the Hardwick Road for a mile. At the roundabout straight over onto A148 through South Gates that leads you on to London Road
CONTACT TEL. NUMBERS	Our Lady of the Annunciation London Road King's Lynn Norfolk Tel. 01553 772220
EMAIL ADDRESS	djjf@btopenworld.com
WEB SITE	www.catholicparish-kingslynn.org.uk
TIMES OF SERVICES	MASS Saturday 6pm Sunday 8am, 11.15am
SPECIAL DATES/ EVENTS/ FESTIVALS/ PILGRIMAGES	No specific, but would be delighted to welcome groups. Mass can be arranged: please phone first
ANGLICAN CHURCH AND CONTACT TEL. NUMBERS	All Saints All Saints Street King's Lynn Norfolk Tel. 01553 771779
LOCAL ATTRACTIONS	Greyfriars Tower (The leaning tower of Lynn, as featured in the final of BBC's 'Restoration' series, September 2003) Red Mount Chapel, The Walks, King's Lynn (inside not open) St Margaret's Benedictine Priory
GOOD PUBS	Stuart House Hotel 33 Goodwins Road King's Lynn Norfolk Tel. 01553 772169
PLACES FOR PILGRIMS TO STAY	Tourist Information Centre Custom House, Purfleet Quay, King's Lynn Tel. 01553 763044

15

Lanherne

LANHERNE

In Celtic times, Cornwall was considered to have had more saints than almost any other part of the country. Like many places in Cornwall, the manor of Lanherne takes its name from a saint; in this case, St Hernan who came here to join the Celtic hermit St Mergeant, from whom the nearby village of St Mawgan takes its name. Lanherne would thus have indicated that this was 'the church of Hernan' – the word 'Lan' meaning church. In later centuries, this area was familiar territory to pilgrims en route from Wales to the Spanish shrine of St James at Compostela.

The manor of Lanherne is situated at the end of one of the longest valleys in Cornwall, two miles from the Atlantic coast. In winter the sound of the waves breaking on the shore carries up the valley, but in summer the atmosphere is one of peace and seclusion, the cattle standing in pools by the streams and anglers searching for the trout that dart into the shadows beneath the river banks. Throughout the centuries Lanherne has been a place set apart in this far-away valley, and there is a timeless quality as the newly-arrived Franciscans take up their mission here at the beginning of the third millennium.

In a windswept landscape scattered with butterfly-like windmills, the road descends through deep woodland into the village of St Mawgan. The Falcon pub on the south side of the road draws its name from the years of persecution, when a falcon would be released to indicate that Mass was about to be celebrated at the manor of Lanherne.

A small gate opens on to a path beneath a canopy of leaves, and as it winds up a steep hill there is an intriguing glimpse of Lanherne Manor with its mullioned windows and mellow stone walls.

On the day of our visit in spring, the scent of wild garlic filled the air, and the path was lined with primroses and early campion. We were warmly welcomed by a Franciscan friar who was busy watering an army of plants and seedlings by the front door. He was clearly an enthusiastic gardener and explained that he had just planted new roses in front of the statue of Our Lady of Lourdes.

We left him quietly tending his plants, and followed the lane that rises past the south of the manor. Still climbing, but sheltered by high walls on either side, the path curves round behind the house, past enclosed kitchen gardens and orchards until one can look down on the magnificent roof of the manor below. Beneath overhanging eaves, the exquisite leadwork is intricately imprinted with the armorial bearings of the Arundell family who lived at Lanherne Manor for nearly five centuries.

The lane is lined with a series of carved Stations of the Cross. As it turns to descend again, the tip of a thirteenth-century church spire comes suddenly into view through a tracery of leaves. The base of the church nestles snugly into the foot of the hill.

At the Reformation the church passed into Anglican hands, but the Arundell aisle remained the property of the Catholic Arundells, and contains a number of the family memorials. A search in the dark shadows of the church also reveal the brasses of some of the Carmelite nuns who came to Lanherne at the time of the French

Revolution and remained throughout the nineteenth and twentieth centuries.

The Arundells

Lanherne had been the seat of the Arundells from the thirteenth century. Tracing their origins to the Norman invasion, the family were the most respected of Cornish gentry and were referred to as the 'great' Arundells to distinguish them from other branches of the family. In the fifteenth century Chideock Castle in Dorset had passed into their hands, as we saw in a previous chapter. The Arundells of Lanherne and of Chideock showed equal courage and fervour during times of persecution.

Over the years, the family produced outstanding patriots and courageous defenders of their Catholic faith. They were benevolent landowners, supporters of the Royalist cause during the Civil War and martyrs for their faith. In each generation, the eldest son was named John. In 1379, the sailor, Sir John Arundell, gathered a fleet of Cornishmen to repulse the French fleet. The invaders turned tail, but Sir John lost his life in the Irish Sea. In 1427 his grandson founded the Arundell chantry of the Blessed Virgin in the nearby church of St Columb which has recently been restored.

There was something quixotic about the Arundells, for they were rarely on the winning side. Generations of the family suffered years of imprisonment, punitive fines, and the sequestration of their land; finally in 1653 Sir John Arundell recovered his estate on payment of a fine of nearly £3,000. With the marriage in 1739 of Sir John's great-granddaughter Mary to the seventh Baron Arundell of Wardour the two families were united, and the association with Lanherne gradually faded. Theirs is a story of heroism and adventure and above all of Christian faith, and at Lanherne there are constant reminders of their presence.

At the time of the Reformation, emissaries of Thomas Cromwell ensured that life for Catholics was difficult and often dangerous. Lanherne Manor, with its broad chimney stacks and rambling passages, became a haven for priests brought over from the English seminary at Douai. They would land in secret coves and travel to the shelter of Lanherne and the hospitality of Sir John Arundell from whence these priests could travel incognito to care for their flocks in the surrounding area. Little is known of the working life of such men. The quest for safe Mass centres was a priority, and the local tin mines running deep into the hillsides may well have provided the necessary 'safe houses' for hiding statues and other 'forbidden' objects as well as for the celebration of Mass. This possibility has been strengthened by the recent discovery of a large piece of driftwood which was washed up on the beach at St Agnes, a few miles from Lanherne. The wood has been identified as an ancient carving of the Blessed Virgin bearing the word *Gaudete*, 'Rejoice'. It is thought that the wooden carving came from the ancient tin mine nearby, flushed out by recent flooding following unusually torrential storms.

Throughout the years following the Dissolution the Arundells continued to harbour priests at Lanherne, although they were under constant threat of discovery. While riding home one day in 1577, a member of the family came upon the severed head of the Cornish martyr, Father Cuthbert Mayne, placed for all to see after he had been hanged, drawn and quartered. A frequent visitor to Lanherne, Father Mayne had been captured at Probus and martyred at Launceston, the first of the seminary priests from Douai to suffer martyrdom in England. Father Cuthbert was canonized in 1970, and his skull remains at Lanherne, contained in a precious reliquary given by Charles Weld of Chideock. It was venerated in public for the first time in 1887.

To the right of the manor the small chapel contains a sanctuary lamp bearing the Arundell crest of swallows: a play on the French word for swallow, *hirondelle*. Although the present chapel dates only from the nineteenth century, there is a tradition that the lamp has not been extinguished since before the Reformation.

After the departure of the Arundells of Lanherne at the end of the sixteenth century, the manor was unoccupied for nearly two hundred years, save for a few brief intervals. Throughout these years, three rooms in the north-east corner of the house were used as a refuge by priests who continued to celebrate Mass, as had been the case since Celtic times. The property eventually fell into the hands of local smugglers, although it remained in the possession of the Arundells of Wardour. In 1794 they handed it over to a small group of English Carmelite nuns, who had been living in the Netherlands but fled to England to escape the French Revolutionary Army which was attacking the Low Countries. The mother prioress, Elizabeth Maddocks, gratefully accepted the offer of Lanherne for herself and fifteen members of her community. It is said that one of the smugglers was still in residence when the Carmelites arrived at Lanherne. He reacted with some surprise at the sight of a nun.

While Englishmen had travelled to Douai to be trained in the priesthood, English women were engaged in founding convents on the Continent. At the beginning of the seventeenth century there had been three English Carmelite foundations in the Netherlands in and around the city of Antwerp, including one in Lierre. At this time, the Carmelites received a small carved statue which was known as Our Lady of Sichem, the gift of the Infanta Isabella, joint Governor of the Netherlands with her husband, the Austrian Archduke Albert. The Carmelites carried the statue with them on their flight to England and, on their arrival at Lanherne, created a shrine in honour of the Blessed Virgin in which they placed the figure of Our Lady of Sichem. This was believed to be the first shrine created in England since the flight of the Catholic James II in 1688.

Amongst the few possessions that the Carmelites brought with them to England were ten portraits of the English martyrs. These had been the gift of Mary Giffard of the Staffordshire branch of the family, who had joined the Carmelites as Sister Mary of the English Martyrs. The Giffard family were instrumental in the escape of Charles II after the battle of Worcester and later gave the land on which the shrine of Our Lady of Brewood was created.

The statue of Our Lady of Sichem was revered at Lanherne for two centuries until the nuns left the manor in 2001. As the statue had been a personal gift, the Carmelites took it with them to their monastery at Ecclestone on Merseyside.

With the arrival of the friars, the tradition of devotion to the Blessed Virgin which has been part of the history of Lanherne has taken a different direction. In addition to the traditional vows of poverty, obedience and chastity, this congregation known as the Franciscan Friars and Sisters of the Immaculate make an additional vow to advance devotion to the Immaculate Heart of Mary throughout the world.

Although the statue of Our Lady of Sichem is no longer present, the Franciscans have replaced her with a statue of the Blessed Virgin dressed in blue and carrying the Holy Child in her arms. On the lawn in front of the manor, a small grotto contains a statue of Our Lady of Lourdes which continues to be a focus of pilgrimage and prayer.

Beyond the chapel is a small enclosed garden with a fine cross made with stone from Pentewan on the south Cornish coast. Beside the cross are the gravestones of several of the Carmelite nuns of Lanherne, carved from slate from the Delabole quarry to the north. Flower beds are filled with wild strawberries, ferns and large sprawling roses surrounded by lady's mantle.

Standing in this tranquil valley beside the ancient manor where prayer has been offered since the sixth century, it is difficult to recall the years of flight and persecution when the manor was filled with adventurous Arundells. Then followed centuries of near silence until the smugglers gave way to the Carmelites who renewed the praise of God in this holy place.

The pageant of history fades into comparative unimportance in this peaceful place where the life of prayer continues uninterrupted.

Shrine – Lanherne

LOCATION/ DIRECTIONS	From M25 Exit J15, M4 Westbound M5 South, A30 to Bodmin A389 Wadebridge A39/A3059 towards Newquay Airport Ignore 1st turning to St Mawgan, take the 2nd turning on the right, past the airport parking area. Travel down steep hill, high stone wall on right (Monastery boundary); take a sharp right into the entrance of the Monastery.
CONTACT TEL. NUMBERS	Franciscans of the Immaculate St Joseph and St Anne Convent St Mawgan in Pydar Newquay Cornwall TR8 4ER Tel. 01637 860205
EMAIL ADDRESS	joseph@ffi-uk.fsnet.co.uk a.diaz1@btinternet.com
TIMES OF SERVICES	Daily Mass 8am Sunday 10am
SPECIAL DATES/ EVENTS/FESTIVALS/ PILGRIMAGES	Pilgrimages at any time by arrangement
ANGLICAN CHURCH AND CONTACT TEL. NUMBERS	St Mawgan-in-Pydar Lanherne (opposite the entrance to monastery) Tel. 01637 860358 www.stmawgan.org.uk
LOCAL ATTRACTIONS	Japanese Gardens and Bonsai Nursery in village (admission charge) www.thebonsainursery.com Stunning scenic coastal walks
GOOD PUBS	Falcon Inn, (opposite entrance to Monastery) St Mawgan Tel. 01637 860225
PLACES FOR PILGRIMS TO STAY	Accommodation available at the Falcon Inn

LINCOLN

16

Lincoln

During the Middle Ages Our Lady was chosen as the patroness of the city of Lincoln, which was described as the most Marian city in the most Marian county of England. In the centuries following the Dissolution, devotion to Mary seemed to be lost beyond recall in this city but against all odds the shrine of Our Lady of Lincoln has been revived.

The River Witham flows south of the city, barges drift past, and this once must have been a pleasant place to linger and enjoy the river with its wild life and the bustle of water traffic. Much of the riverside is now overshadowed by the looming walls of supermarkets and 1970s office blocks.

We walked beside what remains of the water's edge, past children feeding the swans, and along a pedestrian way that led to Stonebow. This medieval stone arch was once the entrance to the city, a place where visitors might pause to greet Our Lady and the Angel Gabriel, as they made their way up the steep hill to the magnificent cathedral. On one side of the arch of Stonebow stands the crowned figure of the Blessed Virgin, her hands folded in prayer as she treads the serpent beneath her feet. On the other side is the Angel Gabriel, holding the remains of the scroll which once bore the opening words of the Hail Mary in Latin: *Ave, gratia plena, Dominus tecum.* The two figures survived the iconoclasm of the sixteenth century, and stand today looking down on the crowds who walk beneath and may sometimes glance up at these figures who have witnessed the comings and going of six centuries.

Through the arch there is an area of shops and coffee bars whose patrons spill into the street to enjoy the sun. The road becomes narrower and steepens for the climb up the hill to the cathedral. There are fewer people now, and those who brave the heat and the hill are clinging to the cool shadows of the old buildings. Some yards further on, the road becomes a lane and finally opens out into a large square. The castle is to the left. Across the square, and through an archway into the cathedral close, we find ourselves facing the magnificent west front of Lincoln Cathedral.

Hugh of Lincoln

The cathedral was built in the eleventh century and dedicated in honour of Our Lady of the Annunciation. In 1186 Lincoln Cathedral had been without a bishop for a number of years when King Henry II summoned the Carthusian prior of Witham in Somerset to fill the vacant see. Hugh of Witham was already renowned, and the King had orginally secured his services as prior of the first Carthusian house in England.

Shortly before St Hugh's arrival in his see, an earthquake rocked the city. The citizens of Lincoln realized that they had a practical man for their bishop when Hugh took up a hod of bricks and set about repairs.

Hugh became much loved in the city, and in the surrounding countryside he became known as the patron of hunters. Local farmers allowed poor men in search of food to trap wild animals on their land. If, however, the King's men caught a man setting traps he would be cruelly treated and sometimes put to death. Those captured frequently suffered trial-by-water, a form of rough justice in which there were no winners. Innocence was 'proved' if one drowned, while the ability to float was considered evidence of guilt. Arrests were carried out on the command of the King's forester. Hugh thought ill of such draconian measures and on one occasion he intervened to ensure that the King's forester was himself arrested and held captive.

St Hugh's devotion to the Blessed Virgin was renowned. He was known as 'Our Lady's most devout servant and vicar', and it said that during his episcopate the cathedral glowed with the light of thousands of tapers burning constantly before the shrine. The blaze of candles in the night was said to give as much light as that which shone by day.

Hugh steadfastly defended the liberty of the Church and yet he managed to remain friends with his monarchs: King Henry II, King Richard I and King John. When he died in the year 1200 two monarchs were pallbearers: John of England and William of Scotland. He was canonized by Pope Honorius only twenty years later, and the fame and popularity of this holy bishop ensured that his shrine in the cathedral became a celebrated place of pilgrimage

THE CLOISTER
LINCOLN CATHEDRAL

Today there are reminders of him throughout Lincoln.

The shrine statue of Our Lady of Lincoln, so greatly honoured by St Hugh, was described by the seventeenth-century Herald and antiquary Sir William Dougdale as 'A great image of Our Lady, sitting in a chair of silver and gilt with four polls, two of them having arms in the front, having upon her head a crown, silver and gilt, set with stones and pearls ... and her Child sitting upon her knee.'

These two great shrines, dedicated to Our Lady of Lincoln and to St Hugh, were rich with jewels and decorations given by the people of Lincoln and pilgrims who came from far and wide. In 1541 Henry VIII arrived in Lincoln with his fifth wife, Katherine Howard. As they processed through the cathedral Henry's eyes fell upon the treasures. Shortly afterwards they were seized and taken away. Nothing is known of the fate of the statue of Our Lady of Lincoln, or of the remains of St Hugh.

One statue of Mary survived the ravages of the Reformation. High up on the exterior of the east-facing wall of the cathedral there stands the last remaining image of Our Lady of Lincoln, dating from the fourteenth century.

When we reached Lincoln on a glorious July day, the green spire of the Catholic church of Our Lady of Lincoln was gleaming in the sun. Built in the 1960s, the new church is light and spacious. In the Lady chapel, to the right of the main altar, there stands the statue of the Blessed Virgin holding the Holy Child as if offering him to the world. The parish began its life after the Second World War in a wooden hut which was rapidly outgrown. In 1943 the parish of Our Lady of Lincoln was separated from that of St Hugh's to the south. The shrine parish also includes villages to the north and east of the city.

In the shrine chapel I fell into conversation with a mild-mannered man who mentioned in passing that he was a prolific writer of crime novels; his work seemed in bizarre contrast to the peace surrounding us, and I left him as he lit candles before the statue of the Blessed Virgin. Her patronage in Lincoln is indeed a reality once more in this busy parish working with Christians of differing denominations in the city.

Shrine – Lincoln

LOCATION/ DIRECTIONS	From M25 Exit J21 M1 Exit J21a A46 to Lincoln Take the B1226 Riseholme Road Turn left on to Skopwick Place and right into Laughton Way (the church is a 1 mile walk from the cathedral)
CONTACT TEL. NUMBERS	The Roman Catholic Church of Our Lady of Lincoln Laughton Way Ermine Estate Lincoln LN2 2HE Tel. 01522 522971 St Hugh of Lincoln Broadgate, Lincoln Tel. 01522 528961
EMAIL ADDRESS	Parish@ourladyoflincoln.fsnet.co.uk
TIMES OF SERVICES	MASS Mon/Tue 9.15am Wed/Thur 9.45am Friday 7.30pm Saturday 10.00am, 6.30pm (Vigil) Sunday 9.30am and 11.00am
ROSARY GROUP	Last Tuesday each month at Lincoln Cathedral
ANGLICAN CHURCH AND CONTACT TEL. NUMBERS	St John the Baptist Church Ermine Tel. 01522 525621 Guided tours are available to discover this unique and important twentieth-century church with its stunning wall of stained glass.
LOCAL ATTRACTIONS	Lincoln Cathedral www.lincolncathedral.com St Mary's Minster, Stow (dedicated to Our Lady) dates back to 1000 www.churchtourism.org. for an excellent Church Trail around Lincoln

GOOD PUBS	Many cafés, pubs and restaurants in the city centre
PLACES FOR PILGRIMS TO STAY	The Lincoln Hotel (overlooks the cathedral) Eastgate Tel. 0871 220 6070 www.thelincolnhotel.com

17

Osmotherley

OSMOTHERLEY

The A19 cuts a swathe through the fields and woodland of north Yorkshire, taking us towards the wonderful abbeys of Rievaulx and Byland, and on to Whitby with its cliff-top monastery. In medieval times this was a northern stronghold of monasticism and the dwelling-place of many Yorkshire saints, among them Aelred of Rievaulx and Chad of Lastingham. There was a rumour that the sixteenth-century martyr, Margaret Clitherow, might lie buried above the village of Osmotherley, in the chapel of Our Lady of Mount Grace.

We reached Osmotherley on a cool spring day, and drove through the village, past the stone on which John Wesley stood and preached in 1745, and beyond that the Queen Catherine pub, before arriving at 18 North End. There has been a small friary in the village since 1665, shortly after the Restoration of Charles II, and today Benedictine monks from nearby Ampleforth Abbey live here and care for the parish and the shrine.

An arch in the stone wall beside the house opens on to a garden, and across the lawn a staircase leads up to a small chapel which continued in use throughout the penal times, and was reordered forty years ago.

Osmotherley is a small village with wide grassy swards fronting cottage gardens which were filled with daffodils on this spring day. As we passed the last of the cottages and turned into Rueberry Lane we began to climb a stony path, pausing occasionally to take in the breathtaking views across the Cleveland Hills.

The lane steadily rises past newly-installed Stations of the Cross, and at the summit of the hill a gateway opens onto a sward of grass. Across this lawn a small chapel of yellow stone attached to a cottage stands in the shelter of a thicket of trees, like an eagle's nest resting above the dramatic descent to the valley below. On closer examination, the remains of the original walls of the chapel appear to have been constructed of large stones on which the graffiti of an earlier age can still be seen; the initials of pilgrims, remnants of prayers and the insignia of those who have travelled to the Holy Land. The smaller stones which were used for the restoration of the chapel in 1959 perfectly match those originally used; they were found amongst the remains of Rosedale Abbey by Fred Handley, a builder from nearby Helmsley who undertook the work.

Beneath this eyrie and obscured by the wooded hillside there lie the ruins of the great Charterhouse of Mount Grace. On this bright spring afternoon the sense of history was tangible in this tiny chapel, in which prayers have been said and candles lit since the fifteenth century. Even when the chapel was reduced to ruins, people still came here to honour the memory of Our Lady of Mount Grace. Some seven centuries later, pilgrimages are once again taking place during the summer months.

The area was once the territory of the powerful northern families of the fourteenth century, and the land was part of the Ingleby estates. A licence was granted in 1397 for the celebration of Mass in John Ingleby's manor house nearby. A holy spring was known to exist on the heights of Mount Grace, and it is possible that the original intention was to build a Carthusian house above the valley, for the land had been levelled here at some time.

However, a year later the Charterhouse of Mount Grace was established in the valley below in honour of the Assumption of Our Lady in Mount Grace – the name suggesting that the spring on the hill above was already known as a place where the Blessed Virgin was honoured. Carthusian monks frequently climbed the 'lady steps' leading up to the spring.

The isolation of this spot held an irresistible lure for those monks who sought the refuge of a hidden place surrounded by the elements and far from human distraction, to listen in silence to the words of the Spirit in a more personal way. A little chapel was established for the monks' use in 1480.

In due course a hermitage was built and in 1515 a hermit arrived whose story has never been forgotten. Thomas Parkinson was born in Bedale in 1488, and married his wife Agnes when he was twenty years old. Their only child was stillborn and was buried in a field nearby in a shallow grave which was uncovered by a raven shortly afterwards. Overwhelmed with grief, the couple decided to separate and retire to a life of prayer, each with the Franciscans. At the behest of Queen Catherine of Aragon, Thomas was installed in the hermitage at Mount Grace where he stayed until the Dissolution. From thence forward he wandered from one misfortune to another, a lost soul always seeking to rediscover the tranquillity of his earlier life. He had, however, established a Franciscan presence at Mount Grace which was to be refounded at Osmotherley many centuries afterwards. His precious time of happiness in the little hermitage, which he owed in part to his queen, is remembered in the name of one of the village pubs. Before the Reformation, many public houses bore the name of Queen Catherine of Aragon. Following the Dissolution most of them renamed themselves as 'the Cat and Fiddle'. Osmotherley is one of the few to have kept the original name.

Despite a waiting-list of men anxious to join the community, the Carthusian priory was closed at the time of the Dissolution, and the monks vanished into the local population. Before departing, the last prior had the presence of mind to endow one of his relations with the chapel of Mount Grace, thereby removing it from church ownership and thus from the danger of destruction. Even this did not stop the chapel gradually falling into ruin but, despite the turbulence of the times, the memory of this isolated shrine was kept alive, and for the first time it became a place of pilgrimage.

In 1569 the Northern Rebellion took place. The northern earls embarked on an ill-fated protest, incensed by the punitive laws that banished the old religion. They had been inspired by the flight of Mary Queen of Scots into England where she was now imprisoned by her cousin, Queen Elizabeth.

The events of the rising led by Thomas Percy, seventh Earl of

Northumberland and Charles Neville, sixth Earl of Westmorland, cannot fail to have affected those living close to Mount Grace, not least when Christopher Neville, son of the fourth Earl of Westmorland, passed by on his way to gather his tenants at Kirbymoorside to join the fray. Failure was almost inevitable and many of the participants suffered torture and death in the aftermath. The severity of legislation that followed the Northern Rising resulted in yet more bloodshed. In York no less than twenty-eight priests were executed and on 25 March 1586 St Margaret Clitherow shared their fate.

Margaret was born in about 1553 to one Thomas Middleton, a wax chandler, and at the age of eighteen she married John Clitherow of the city of York. Shortly afterwards she became a Catholic and in her new-found faith, she gave constant support and refuge to priests who passed through the area. In 1575 Margaret was imprisoned for two years for failing to attend the services of the Anglican church. Eleven years later a search of the Clitherow home in York's Shambles produced evidence considered to be sufficient for her arrest.

Wishing to spare her children and servants the anguish of giving evidence at her trial, Margaret refused to plead. Such refusal carried the absolute penalty of *peine forte et dure*, in accordance with a law of the reign of King Henry IV. On 25 March 1586 Margaret Clitherow was crushed to death, a stone beneath her spine and a door weighed down by heavy stones placed upon her body. She was canonized in 1970 and in the Shambles a shrine in her honour has been created.

The order was given that her burial should be carried out swiftly in an obscure part of the city, and for six weeks her friends and family searched for the body in vain. When finally discovered the corpse was 'as fair and clear as though she had been but new dead' according to a contemporary account. A decision was taken concerning the final resting place of the martyr, but the burial place was never revealed. At nightfall the body was taken secretly by horse on 'a long journey' and given Christian burial. There is a tradition that Mount Grace may have been the chosen place.

York lies some thirty miles from Mount Grace and the journey, if undertaken under cover of darkness, would certainly qualify as 'long' and there could be no doubt that it was dangerous. The remoteness of Mount Grace would not have escaped those seeking a place, not merely of safety, but in which some form of watch might be kept on so precious a grave. This little chapel was rarely without pilgrims who managed to create a thread of continuity in

AMPLEFORTH ABBEY

a changing world in which so many monasteries and nunneries had been abandoned. The men and women who trod the steep hill up to Our Lady's shrine would surely have spared a prayer for the repose of the soul of Margaret Clitherow as she rested in a peace so richly deserved. A tantalizing question mark remains, however tempting such speculation may be.

At the end of the sixteenth century, the roofs of the chapel were removed to discourage pilgrims, and it had fallen into ruin – but still the pilgrims came. On 7 September 1614 sixteen people were arrested, amongst them a relation of the Clitherow family, and several children, all of whom had come to pray at Mount Grace on the day before the feast of Our Lady's Birthday. On the York castle prison list of 1619 several of their names appear, including that of Margaret Clitherow's stepson, William.

Among those who visited the chapel and the holy spring some years later was Mary Ward, foundress of the Institute of the Blessed Virgin Mary. Her religious sisters had already journeyed to the shrine to pray for her recovery from serious illness, and in 1642 Mary Ward came in person to give thanks for her restored health.

The Franciscan legacy of the hermit, Thomas Parkinson, eventually came to fruition in 1665, when a Franciscan friary was established in the house at 18 North End which is presently occupied by Benedictines. Here the Franciscans remained for 167 years.

After their departure in 1832 the Friary chapel was almost forgotten and regarded as lost to the Catholic cause; however, pilgrims continued to make their way up the increasingly overgrown lane to the Lady chapel, especially on feast days of the Blessed Virgin. Gradually the remaining walls disintegrated, concealed in a tangle of weeds and encroaching woodland, and the site was abandoned to the ravages of nature.

On a June day in 1942, two young priests, Father Peter Storey and Father Michael O'Sullivan, bicycled away from Middlesbrough Cathedral and out into the countryside towards Osmotherley. Father Peter had seen marked on the map 'lady chapel (ruin)' and they had decided to explore. Having eaten their picnic among the ruins of Mount Grace Priory, the two priests climbed the steep hill, clambering over walls and hedges, until they reached the brow, where they saw before them the ruined chapel with the abandoned cottage beside it. By the time that the two young men scrambled down the hill they had determined that they must find out more about the Lady chapel of Mount Grace. This was a turning point in the story of the shrine, and the awakened interest brought about the revival of its fortunes, not least in the learned research carried out by Father Peter's brother, Father Anthony Storey, which resulted in the publication of his book, *Mount Grace Lady Chapel* published by Highgate Publications (Beverley) Limited, in 2001.

Although several years passed before restoration was possible, the renewed interest stirred local memories. In the years following the First World War, the cottage adjoining the ruined chapel had been inhabited despite its lack of any amenity, and the ruins had become a kitchen garden. Nevertheless, the Marist fathers managed to celebrate Mass amongst the vegetation in the chapel ruins shortly after the war. And pilgrims continued to climb the hill, now in ever greater numbers, to pray before what remained of the ruins and the spring which is now below the ground beyond the corner of the cottage.

Faced with heavy taxation on his Ingleby estates, Sir Hugh Bell approached Father Peter in 1954 with an informal offer to sell the cottage, the ruin and the Chapel Wood. Father Peter turned to Mr Ralph Scrope who was land agent to the Earl and Countess of Eldon. The two families decided to purchase the property together; the terms were rapidly agreed and the sale was completed. The chapel was restored, and in 1958 the first diocesan pilgrimage was held: this is now an annual event.

The Crucifix in the Lady chapel was a gift from Lady Eldon. She had seen it hanging in an antique shop in Germany in the early nineteen-thirties and decided that she wished to acquire it. The owner of the shop was Jewish and already suffering under the Nazi regime. He offered the Cross to Lady Eldon as a gift in return for her assistance with his immigration into England. This she duly arranged and her precious reward now hangs above the altar and is a reminder of the holocaust and of one man's freedom.

On the west window of the Lady chapel are the four shields of the benefactors; the arms of Queen Catherine of Aragon, and those of Sir James Strangways, who willed in 1522 that priests should sing their prayer for the repose of his soul, and who endowed the chapel accordingly. His wife, Alice, was the daughter of the fifth Earl of Masham from whom Ralph Scrope Esq was descended. Mr Scrope's arms are quartering the arms of his wife, Beatrice Savile, daughter of the sixth Earl of Mexborough together with the arms of the fourth Earl of Eldon quartering the arms of his wife, Magdalen Fraser, daughter of the fourteenth Lord Lovat.

The grounds are now carefully maintained; there are frequent pilgrimages to the restored chapel, and the cottage is let for short stays in the summer. In 1961 Cardinal William Godfrey of Westminster blessed the restored chapel, and four years later the Franciscans returned to their little house in Osmotherley. Further restoration was carried out, and in 1985 a Blessed Sacrament chapel was built on the foundations of the old hermitage, with a small cloister connecting it to the Lady chapel. In 1993 the friars departed, and the Benedictines of Ampleforth Abbey became responsible for Mount Grace.

The trees on the hill behind the Lady chapel were almost all planted by Father Peter Storey or his brother, Father Anthony Storey. As a memorial to them, and to all involved in the restoration of the Lady chapel, a path has been laid through the trees to a quiet meditative place with stunning panoramic views at the very summit of the hill. In 2003, the year of the Rosary, work began on the path which was the result of a unique partnership between the Benedictines, the North York Moor National Park, and the inmates at Kirklevington Grange Prison. As so often in its history, the Lady chapel continues to speak to people of many different backgrounds and varying needs.

When we arrived with the Prior, we walked through the Lady chapel and into the Blessed Sacrament chapel. The pews were carved by the firm of Robert Thompson of Kilburn and include his famous mouse emblem. Next door is an excellent shop and a meeting room which can be used as an extension to the chapel.

On the wall of the meeting room is a large tapestry of Our Lady of the Tatra Mountains in Poland. This was a gift of the Polish people to the diocese of Middlesbrough in thanksgiving for the medicines and clothing that were delivered to Poland in the years leading up to the fall of the Berlin Wall.

Somewhat incongruously, the room includes a closed-circuit television to enable services in the chapel next door to be transmitted. We turned on a switch to see how it worked, and stood transfixed. The camera did indeed show the altar of the chapel, and there before us was a small boy struggling to dislodge the box of meagre offerings from beneath the candles. This appears to be a common occurrence, and the priests are guardians of the chapel in more senses than one.

We turned to make our way down the lane in the evening light, leaving this little chapel which has withstood the passage of time. In the winter months, there are fewer visitors to the Lady chapel, and one is reminded of the silent refuge sought by hermits so long ago, but in the summer the chapel of Mount Grace is visited by a constant stream of walkers and pilgrims – and even small boys in search of extra pocket money.

Shrine – Osmotherley – Mount Grace

LOCATION/ DIRECTIONS	From M25, exit J21 M1, exit J32 M18, exit J2 A1(M), Exit for A168/A19 towards Thirsk Continue for 9 miles and turn right for Osmotherley Leave your car in the village and walk due North in the direction of Swainby. After about 300m from the centre of the village, on the left-hand side of the road, is the beginning of Rueberry Lane. It is also indicated by a Cleveland Way signpost. Follow Rueberry Lane for about one mile up a steep rough track, bearing right at the fork, and you will arrive at the chapel. *Please note that there is no public right of way for motor vehicles along Rueberry Lane. Visitors should have adequate footwear to tackle the walk.*
CONTACT TEL. NUMBERS	The Monastery of Our Lady of Mount Grace 18 North End Osmotherley Northallerton North Yorkshire Tel. 01609 883308
EMAIL ADDRESS	t.richardson@freeuk.com ladychapel@btconnect.com
WEB SITE	www.ladychapel.org.uk
TIMES OF SERVICES	Mass is celebrated in the Lady Chapel:- Every Saturday at 3.30pm, evening prayer follows at about 4.40pm, and on Lady Days – contact Monastery for details 1st Friday month – service of Word and Holy Communion followed by Exposition of Blessed Sacrament 3pm Sacrament of Reconciliation Saturday 2.45pm – 3.15pm

SPECIAL DATES/ EVENTS/ FESTIVALS/ PILGRIMAGES	1st Bank Holiday in May, Benedictine Pilgrimage July, Reparation-Consecration Pilgrimage at Osmotherley July, Ecumenical Pilgrimage to Lady chapel Sunday nearest August 15th the Assumption Pilgrimage 1st Sunday of October, the Rosary Pilgrimage Last Sunday of every month, Pilgrimage for Peace There are many more events at the Lady chapel; please contact for more details. Groups are very welcome, by arrangement
ROSARY GROUP	Silent Meditation Group, Mondays 7.30pm
ANGLICAN CHURCH AND CONTACT TEL. NUMBERS	St Peter's Osmotherley Tel. 01274 541948
LOCAL ATTRACTIONS	North Yorkshire Moors National Park. Mount Grace Priory (English Heritage/NT) Tel. 01609 883494 Thorp Perrow Arboretum, near Bedale www.thorpperrow.com
GOOD PUBS	Several pubs, cafés in village
PLACES FOR PILGRIMS TO STAY	A cottage is available, tel. 01609 833808 or Osmotherley Youth Hostel nearby, tel. 01609 883575

18

Prinknash

The magnificent situation of this monastery must be one of the glories of England and brings to mind the words of Gerard Manley Hopkins: 'The world is charged with the grandeur of God'.

The first Benedictine monks to establish an abbey in Gloucester arrived in the eleventh century at the behest of King Canute. As they crested the Cotswold escarpment above the plain that unfolds to the blue hills of the Forest of Dean and to Wales in the distance these men can rarely have experienced such evidence of the Creator in his creation.

Nine hundred years later the view is little changed. On a fine day in May we arrived at the monastery of Prinknash (pronounced Prinnich) beneath a sky laden with scudding clouds and showers; a watery sun cast pools of light in the shadows on the lane and on the leaves of overhanging beech trees. After a steep climb we reached the crest of the hill and gazed down past the monastery to the spectacular tapestry of fields and hills that fall away to the city of Gloucester far below.

On entering the gates of the monastery, the drive descends steeply through an avenue of chestnut trees to the large car park beside the Visitor Centre.

Gloucester

In the early years of the eleventh century, monastic life must have been harsh indeed and it appears to have almost defeated the Benedictines in Gloucester. When William the Conqueror appointed the first Norman abbot, some fifty years after the arrival of the first community, the monastery was described as being nearly defunct.

But with the arrival of Abbot Serlo, building began immediately. The abbot and his community wasted no time in starting work on land which is now in the precincts of Gloucester Cathedral. In the year 1100 the abbey church, now the cathedral, was consecrated and named in honour of St Peter. The speed with which this magnificent building rose from the ground is breathtaking and the skill of the builders remains a constant source of wonder.

By the thirteenth century, a new Lady chapel had replaced an earlier edifice. For the next three hundred and fifty years, devotions in honour of the Blessed Virgin were very much a part of the liturgical life of the abbey of St Peter. The Lady chapel stands behind the high altar of Gloucester Cathedral with walls that appear to be made entirely of glass. Although the altar screen bears the scars of the Reformers' axe, the figures of the saints are still in evidence and seem to gather around the statue of Our Lady.

In 1096 land which spread far to the south of the abbey came into the hands of the monks, in an act of generosity on the part of the Giffard family that was to ensure that their name would be remembered for ever in the annals of the Benedictines of Gloucester and Prinknash.

The Giffards had come to England with William the Conqueror. In common with many of his Norman companions in arms, they were rewarded with vast tracts of land, much of which the conquerors devoted to the establishment of monasteries. The land at Prinknash was the gift of Heylas Giffard and twenty-five years later, in 1121, his son Elias was to join the community at Gloucester.

In 1096, Giffard's generous benefaction provided the community with valuable farming land upon which they built a mill. The monks must have enjoyed the chase, for soon a hunting lodge was also built. At the beginning of the sixteenth century Abbot Will Parker enlarged this building to such an extent that it became known as the Abbot's Mansion and remained the principal dwelling on the property until the building of the new monastery in 1972.

Dissolution

In July 1535, King Henry VIII and Anne Boleyn left Windsor on a royal progression through Gloucestershire where they remained for a week, and were entertained at Over, near Prinknash, by Abbot Parker.

It is one of the ironic footnotes of history, that on the eve of the royal departure from Windsor for the abbey of Gloucester, Henry's former Lord Chancellor, St Thomas More, was engaged in writing a last letter to his beloved daughter, Margaret from his cell in the Tower of London.

As the King rode away from London on the following morning, his erstwhile Chancellor was executed at the Tower of London. How little could Henry or Thomas More have suspected that four hundred years later a statue of Our Lady which had belonged to More would provide the centerpiece in a restored Benedictine shrine outside Gloucester! In 1535 only the shrewdest of observers could have guessed that the Benedictines would ever leave Gloucester, let alone be deprived of their other English monasteries.

In 1540, only five years after the visit of Henry and Anne Boleyn, the great abbey of Gloucester was suppressed, and the monks pensioned off. In 1541 Henry appointed the last abbot of nearby Tewkesbury as the first bishop of the newly-founded see of Gloucester, with the former abbey church of St Peter as his cathedral.

Caldey

Following the Dissolution, the Prinknash estate passed into private hands. In 1888 it was acquired by Thomas Dyer-Edwardes, a devout Anglican. Thomas transformed the estate, introducing flower gardens and avenues of trees; peacocks strutted across carefully-tended lawns and the stables housed a team of six white mules. As one looks across the abbey lands towards the bird sanctuary and gardens, it is clear that his work was not in vain. He would surely approve of the developments to his park, which is enjoyed today by thousands of visitors.

In 1924 Dyer-Edwardes became a Roman Catholic, and decided that Prinknash should be returned to its former owners. He offered the land to the Benedictine community of Caldey Island, off the coast of South Wales, complete with the Abbot's Mansion, his large and comfortable dwelling. The Benedictine community of Caldey had originally belonged to the Anglican Communion and had a particular devotion to the Virgin Mary. In her honour, they wore white habits rather than the customary Benedictine black. In 1913 almost the entire community asked to be received into the Catholic Church, and sought affiliation to the Benedictine congregation of Subiaco. As a mark of their devotion to Mary, they sought and received the approval of Pope Pius X to continue to wear their distinctive white habits.

In the aftermath of the First World War, the community faced both financial difficulties and a loss of manpower. The offer of Prinknash reached Caldey Island in 1924, at a time of deep concern for Abbot Wilfred Upson, and coincided with an invitation to travel to France to the shrine of Our Lady of Lourdes. In need of rest and reflection, the abbot departed on pilgrimage.

Living in Lourdes in 1925 was Mrs Agnes Sutcliffe who owned a statue, known as the Waterton Madonna, which had belonged to her ancestor, St Thomas More. After More's execution the statue had been hidden, and was then smuggled out of England by members of the family, to remain in exile awaiting more peaceful times. It was now in Mrs Sutcliffe's private chapel in Lourdes.

After celebrating Mass in this chapel, the abbot was greatly surprised by Mrs Sutcliffe's suggestion that he should take this historic statue back to Caldey with him. He had been told of the family's long-standing intention to establish a shrine for the conversion of England, and appreciated that he was being asked to carry out their wishes. Abbot Upson acceded to Mrs Sutcliffe's request, and duly returned to Wales with his precious cargo.

The carved oak statue is almost certainly Flemish in origin. It dates from the late fifteenth century, and traces of the original gilding are visible on the wood. The Holy Child sits on his Mother's left arm, while he holds on to her neck and touches her cheek. The statue frequently wears a lace cloak and fine crowns of silver gilt and precious stones.

On arrival at Caldey the statue was carried in procession to the choir on 18 October 1925, the feast of St Luke and the anniversary of the monks' arrival on the island in 1906. Thus the Waterton Madonna became known as Our Lady of the Choir.

The story of this statue might have rested there but for Thomas Dyer-Edwardes' offer of the Prinknash estate – and even that hung in the balance, for he died before the deed of gift was finalized. The great generosity of his grandson, Lord Rothe, ensured that the transaction went ahead, and Prinknash was returned into Benedictine hands.

In 1928 the monks bade a final farewell to Caldey with heavy hearts, although they were much cheered on their departure by the appearance of a spectacular rainbow above the boat taking them to the mainland. They arrived at Prinknash during one of the coldest winters on record.

The community has flourished since its arrival and two further foundations have been established at Farnborough and Pluscarden. Since 1987 a venture in Sunyani in Ghana has become the work of the whole Province of Subiaco in Great Britain.

When the community reached Prinknash the statue of Our Lady of the Choir, now known as Our Lady of Prinknash, was enshrined in the abbot's chapel, placed in a carved niche beneath a canopy. In the Marian year of 1954, an oak and glass shrine was placed on the lawn in front of the abbey so that the many pilgrims could pray before the statue of Our Lady in the summer sunshine.

In the year 2002 the statue was stolen. On 20 September, between community supper and the evening office of Compline, it vanished, and has yet to be returned. This is a tragedy not only for the Benedictine community of Prinknash, but to all who honour Our Lady in England and keep alive the memory of St Thomas More who loved his country and his king, but loved his Catholic faith better than his life. May the ancient Madonna of Prinknash return one day to this beautiful place, to those who love and revere her.

Shrine – Prinknash

LOCATION DIRECTIONS	From M25, exit J15
	M4 and join M5 Northbound exit J13
	A4096 Stroud
	Take the A46 towards Cheltenham, and Prinknash is on the left just past Painswick
CONTACT TEL. NUMBERS	Prinknash Abbey
	Cranham
	Gloucestershire
	Tel. 01452 812455
EMAIL ADDRESS	paxprinknash@waitrose.com
WEB SITE	www.prinknashabbey.org.uk
TIMES OF SERVICES	MASS
	Weekdays
	as announced
	Holy Days
	Sung (Conventual) Mass 10.30am
	Vespers 6.00pm
	Sundays
	Low Mass 8.15am
	Sung (Conventual) Mass 10.30am
	Vespers 6.00pm
ANGLICAN CHURCH AND CONTACT TEL. NUMBERS	Christ Church
	Gloucester Street, Painswick
	Tel. 01452 814183
LOCAL ATTRACTIONS	Within the abbey grounds you will find The Craft Centre, Orpheus Pavement and The Bird Park.
	Painswick Rococo Garden
	Painswick, Glos.
	Tel. 01452 813204
	www.rococogarden.co.uk

GOOD PUBS

Tearoom and gift shop is open 9.30am to 5.00pm. Light lunches, hot and cold snacks, cream teas.

PLACES FOR PILGRIMS TO STAY

At the time of going to press as the community has relocated to the old monastry, formerly known as St Peter's Grange, no male or female guests can be accomodated until further notice. Please check the website for any future developments. www.pricknashabbey.org.uk

19

Stone

STONE

This waterside town acquired its name in the middle of the seventh
century, when Wulfhere was King of Mercia. At the time of this
story St Chad, abbot of the Yorkshire monastery of Lastingham, had
recently become Bishop of Mercia and was renowned for his
inspired teaching. One day the King went hunting in the forest with

his two sons, Wulfhad and Rufin. They became separated from their father, encountered the bishop, and before long the boys asked to be baptized. In his fury, the King ordered the beheading of his own sons. The Queen, who was a Christian and overcome with grief, ordered that a monument of stone should be erected over the graves of Wulfhad and Rufin. This gave the town its name, and the two young princes are remembered as the Martyrs of Stone.

The town lies between Birmingham and Stoke-on-Trent and beside the Trent and Mersey canal where brightly-coloured barges drift slowly past the towpaths. The approach from the south leads across fields and over the canal to the town which is situated on a hill. At the summit is the church of the Immaculate Conception and St Dominic.

We arrived on a cold winter's day and the wind swept across the fields and whipped around the hilltop – there was no-one to be seen. The church was locked and then, as if from nowhere, a Dominican nun appeared from around the corner and led us to the main entrance of the convent.

The large wooden door opened and we were ushered along a passageway to the waiting room. Childhood memories flooded into my mind of these spotless, barely-used convent parlours, the air laden with the scent of polish and flowers, with the hint of cooking from distant kitchens. Stiff upright chairs always increased the anxiety of waiting.

A tall nun appeared soundlessly before us, the long folds of her habit continuing to unfurl long after her feet had ceased to move, her gentle face wreathed in smiles of welcome. As we followed her, the convent was silent and still, but for the occasional shadow of a nun disappearing around the corner of the cloister.

A labyrinth of sculleries and laundry rooms led eventually to the back door, and we emerged on to paths and lawns. In the distance gardeners were busy in the kitchen garden, and in the centre of the garden the statue of Our Lady of Stone was standing on a small mound, protected by a glass structure. The finely-carved figure of the Blessed Virgin leans protectively over her Son who stands beside her looking down on the globe beneath his feet.

There is a sense of other-worldliness here, created by the presence of the Dominican Sisters of St Catherine of Siena, and yet the convent is also home to a large school, and the parish church of the Immaculate Conception and St Dominic is close by. The convent of St Dominic is thriving at the beginning of the third millennium as the foundress, Mother Margaret Hallahan, intended.

Mother Margaret

When the future bishop of Birmingham, William Ullathorne, set about restoring the fortunes of the Catholic population of Coventry in 1842, he sought the assistance of Margaret Hallahan. She was a remarkable person, and her memory is lovingly venerated by the Dominicans of Stone.

Born in London of Irish parents in 1802, Margaret was orphaned by the age of ten. After some confusion as to what should be done with this child, she found herself in domestic service with an English family who had moved to Belgium, where they lived in the town of Bruges. The loneliness of her childhood thenceforward was made bearable by her great love for the Blessed Virgin. Even today, almost every corner in Bruges has a niche or alcove set high above the street for a statue of Mary and beneath, in summer, there are frequently little pots of scarlet geraniums cheerfully catching the eye.

In a neighbouring village there is a shrine dedicated to Our Lady of Assebroek, and to this chapel Margaret would go each morning, rising at 2 a.m. to attend Mass before returning to Bruges in time to start work. She walked along country lanes to reach Assebroek, which today is submerged in the sprawling suburbs of the city. The figure of Mary is surrounded by a filigree silver decoration of flowers, and a small silver boat beneath reminds the pilgrim of the nearness of the North Sea and of Our Lady's title, *Stella Maris*, Star of the Sea.

Margaret became affiliated to the Dominicans as a member of their Third Order, and in 1835 she was professed. Seven years later the invitation arrived to join Father Ullathorne at Coventry. Before leaving Bruges, she was given a small statue of the Blessed Virgin by her confessor, Father Versaval. The statue had been left to him by a Dutch woman with the express wish that it should be given to someone possessing a deep love of Mary. Today this little figure is treasured by the community at Stone where it is known as Our Lady Refuge of Sinners.

The task of renewing Catholic life in Coventry was immense, and the workload of Margaret Hallahan and her dedicated followers was increased by the addition of a school. While this work was being carried out, Sister Margaret and three companions began their novitiate under the future bishop's direction, and in 1845 the three were professed. Mother Margaret became their Superior and together they formed a community under the title of the Dominican Sisters of St Catherine of Siena which was eventually established in Stone, some eight miles to the north.

During the years following the Reformation, the Catholics of Stone had been able to attend Mass in the private chapel of the Fitzherbert family at nearby Swynnerton. In 1841 Blessed Dominic Barberi, the Italian missionary priest, opened a small mission at Aston Hall, three miles to the south of Stone, and a year later, on land given by Mr James Beech, a small chapel was built in Stone itself in honour of St Anne, the mother of Mary. On the day of our visit, we found this little chapel in a leafy corner of the garden. Although it is now dwarfed by the convent and church buildings that have risen around it, when the designs were completed in 1843 by Augustus Pugin it was a brave statement of a renewed Catholic presence. Pugin had proved that it was possible to create a small chapel which had beauty and proportion, and the little building has a buttressed nave and a chancel of brick with stone dressings. There is a path leading beneath the shade of overhanging trees to this jewel-like building with its cool stone interior. On the altar stands the cross that belonged to Blessed Dominic Barberi and the window behind is dedicated to St Anne.

By the 1850s, the need to find land for a convent for the growing number of those wishing to join the new Dominican congregation was becoming a matter of increasing concern to Mother Margaret. In 1852 James Beech donated the land to build a convent near St Anne's chapel. The foundation stone was laid almost immediately by William Ullathorne, who had now become the first Bishop of Birmingham. In 1853 the nuns moved in.

There were never sufficient funds available for building, but for Mother Margaret this was of little concern, for somehow the money always materialized. This faith in heavenly intervention was proved time and again, and most famously on one of her several visits to Belgium. In 1856 she saw a beautiful four foot oak statue of Our Lady of Victories on display in the Town Hall in Bruges. Mother Margaret knew immediately exactly where it should stand. Although she had no idea how this might actually be accomplished, she 'invited' the Blessed Virgin to come to Staffordshire, where she would be known as Our Lady of Stone.

The 'invitation' was accepted. In 1862 a Dr Spencer Northcote bought the statue, and it was placed within the chapel of St Anne, which remained the shrine of Our Lady of Stone for some ninety years. The doctor's three little children lie buried in the graveyard outside the chapel of St Anne. Before her death in 1868, Mother Margaret had made it known that eventually the figure of Our Lady should stand 'on a mountain' for all to see, adding that if no mountain was available, then initiative should be used in order to create one. A very small mountain was made; it was moved three times before it came to rest in 1953 in its present place in the centre of the garden.

Some months after our first visit to the Dominican convent, we returned as part of a pilgrimage and stood before the statue of Our Lady in this most English of gardens, under the gaze of school children who peered from every window. On this occasion, the sun shone and we were surrounded by the humming of bees among the first flowers of summer.

The day began with the celebration of Mass in the church of St Dominic and of the Immaculate Conception. This handsome church was consecrated in 1863 and is filled with fascinating reminders of Dominican history and of the saints of the Order.

Beside the central section on the main altar, which is decorated with scenes connected with the Blessed Sacrament, a large carving on the right of the altar depicts the death of St Dominic, and on the left is the Assumption of the Blessed Virgin surrounded by Dominican saints: Thomas Acquinas; St Dominic, the founder of the Dominican family; Pope St Pius V, and St Hyacinth. To the left of St Joseph's altar, Bishop Ullathorne lies buried in the transept – Mother Margaret had been determined that he should rest here.

The Incarnation was central to Dominican teaching in the struggle against the Albigensian heresy in the thirteenth century. In acknowledgement of this, the rosary altar is carved with the scene of the Angel Gabriel appearing to the Blessed Virgin Mary. St Dominic is also shown receiving the rosary from the Blessed Virgin.

When our pilgrimage drew to a close, we gathered in the cloister of the convent, and before we departed the prioress, Sister Mary Henry, led us up the staircase to the convent library to show us a little-known shrine of Mary. Sister Mary Henry spoke of the founder of their Order and of the small figure of Our Lady Refuge of Sinners that had travelled with Mother Margaret from Bruges so many years ago, and now stood before us on a desk that had once belonged to Pope St Pius X.

We were aware of the privilege that had been ours in visiting this order of the Dominican Sisters of Saint Catherine of Siena, and we turned reluctantly to leave the figure of Our Lady of Stone on its 'mountain' in the garden, and the lesser-known shrine within the convent.

Shrine – Stone

LOCATION/ DIRECTIONS	From M25, exit J16, M40, M42 North, M6, exit J14 A34 to Stone At roundabout take 3rd exit onto Stafford Street – A520 (signposted Stone) Bear left onto Crown Street. Keep in left-hand lane then continue forword (signposted Newcastle-under-Lyme A34). Bear left onto Newcastle Street – B5027. Turn right onto Margaret Street
CONTACT TEL. NUMBERS	The Immaculate Conception and St Dominic Margaret Street, Stone Staffordshire Tel. 01785 813951 01785 812091 – Convent
EMAIL ADDRESS	mail@stone-dominicans.org.uk
WEB SITE	www.stone-dominicans.org.uk
TIMES OF SERVICES	Daily (Mon–Tues) 10.00am (Wed) 9.00am (Friday) 6pm Vigil for Sunday: 6.00pm Sunday 8.15am, 10.45am Holydays: 9.15am, 7.00pm
SPECIAL DATES/ EVENTS/ FESTIVALS/ PILGRIMAGES	No special dates, but groups and individuals are very welcome; please phone to make prior arrangements
ROSARY GROUP	Every day after Mass
ANGLICAN CHURCH AND CONTACT TEL. NUMBERS	Christ Church Christ Church Way Stone Tel. 01785 812669
LOCAL ATTRACTIONS	Wedgwood Visitor Centre Wedgwood Barlaston, Stoke on Trent
PLACES FOR PILGRIMS TO STAY	Rooms are available for individuals at the Convent

20

Sudbury

SUDBURY

Situated between Clare and Long Melford in Suffolk, Sudbury was originally a Saxon manor but passed into the ownership of the de Clare family after the Conquest. Wherever de Clares were to be found, at Clare, Walsingham, Tewkesbury or Caversham, it was a foregone conclusion that the Blessed Virgin would be held in honour.

The story of the shrine of Our Lady of Sudbury is in fact the story of two churches; the large medieval church of St Gregory and the much later Catholic church of Our Lady and St John the Evangelist. The two stand side by side, like members of the same family; the bigger and older one seems to dominate but, as is the case in many families, it is in fact the vigour and energy of the younger sister that is encouraging the healing of old wounds. There is renewed hope for the restoration of a shared devotion to Our Lady which was once so much a part of the life of Sudbury.

These two churches stand in a beautiful setting beside the Croft, a pleasant greensward beneath large oak trees that runs down to the River Stour, home to innumerable swans and ducks. In pre-Reformation days, a fair was held each year on the Croft between 10 and 12 July – the feast of St Benedict is on 11 July; a Benedictine connection is also to be found in the dedication of the church of St Gregory the Great – Benedictine monk, Pope and Doctor of the Church.

The Catholic church of Our Lady and St John the Evangelist is a fine building designed in 1893 by the architect Leonard Stokes.

The fourteenth-century church of St Gregory is a handsome building with strange idiosyncrasies which make it all the more interesting. It has a double porch which shares its roof with the chapel of Our Lady and St Anne and some of the lower parts of the windows are blocked to prevent the congregation from freezing to death during long sermons. The black and white checked flintwork on the outer walls is superb. Inside the church, blue and gold painted ceilings above the chancel are strewn with stars and guarded by carved angels.

St Gregory's was built by the future Archbishop of Canterbury and Chancellor of England, Simon of Sudbury, who also founded a college for poor priests in the town. Although his magnificent fourteenth-century church still stands, all that remains of his college is a fine medieval arch to one side of the churchyard. Simon was appointed to the see of Canterbury in 1375, and two years later he crowned the young King Richard II. The Archbishop had a mixed career, marked by great achievement, which was somewhat marred when he was seen to be responsible for the unjust taxation which led to the Peasants' Revolt of 1381. He was seized by the mob and beheaded: his skull remains in the church of St Gregory, where it is kept in the vestry cupboard, a rather undignified end for such an august character.

The precise date of the founding of the shrine of Our Lady is not known, although it is presumed to have been during the lifetime of

Simon of Sudbury. Even the exact position of the original statue in the church of St Gregory remains uncertain; it is possible that it stood in a niche in the chancel, which can still be seen. But it is considered more likely that it was situated in the chapel of Our Lady and St Anne to the west end of the south aisle.

The shrine of Our Lady of Sudbury became a popular place of pilgrimage for those on their way either to the shrine of Walsingham or to the shrine of the ninth-century martyr, King Edmund, at Bury St Edmunds. In her household expenses it is recorded that Henry VII's Queen, Elizabeth of York made a gift to the shrine on 24 March 1502.

In pre-Reformation days, the feast of the Assumption on 15 August was known as Our Lady in Harvest, and pilgrimages were part of the celebrations. In Sudbury the procession started at the Benedictine priory of St Bartholomew, from there the statue of Our Lady was carried through the town, surrounded by flags and banners and accompanied by crowds bearing sheaves of corn. The procession ended at St Gregory's Church where Our Lady was returned to her shrine. It was an annual event of great importance and enjoyment, which came to an abrupt end in 1537 with the arrival of the King's Commissioners.

The church was stripped of all objects of piety, and especially of anything associated with the Blessed Virgin and the Saints. The process of stripping continued for over a century, and in 1644 the 'parliamentary visitor' of the Suffolk churches, William Dowsing, boasted of having purged no less than 150 churches of their stained-glass windows and other relics. There is little doubt that St Gregory's Church with its ancient shrine to Our Lady would have been among the first to suffer, and for four hundred years a pall of silence fell upon the shrine of Our Lady of Sudbury.

Restoration

Almost imperceptibly the ancient custom of devotion to Our Lady was renewed in Sudbury with the restoration of the Slipper Chapel at Walsingham in 1934. Pilgrimages wound their way through Suffolk to Norfolk once more, stirring memories of the shrine of Our Lady of Sudbury which had been such an important stopping place on the pilgrim route. The parish priest of Sudbury, Father Gerard Moir, returned from a pilgrimage to Walsingham determined to restore the shrine.

There was no accurate description of the appearance of the original statue in the shrine of Our Lady of Sudbury. Martin Gillett,

OUR LADY OF SUDBURY

of the Ecumenical Society of the Blessed Virgin Mary, asserts that the model for the restored statue was in fact the statue of Our Lady which had been revered in the ancient French Benedictine monastery of Cluny until its suppression in 1790. Gillett does not, however, provide us with a source reference for this claim. Neither does it seem possible to establish the exact appearance of the Cluny statue so many years after its disappearance. Although a Benedictine model for the restored statue would certainly be in keeping with Sudbury's long-standing Benedictine associations through the priory of St Bartholomew and the church dedicated to the Benedictine Pope, St Gregory the Great, there is insufficient evidence to be sure about this.

Father Peter Rollings, parish priest of Sudbury and author of *Walsingham – England's Nazareth*, finds no evidence that the design of the statue had anything to do with Cluny. The statue was made by James and Lilian Dagless who were also responsible for much of the work in the restored Slipper Chapel at Walsingham. Although originally gilded, the Sudbury statue had been decorated in different colours but has recently been restored to the original brilliance. In keeping with the style of other figures of the Blessed Virgin in East Anglia which were modelled upon classic Orthodox iconography, it offers an endearing image of the Mother and an almost playful Child who appears to be tugging at her shawl. Today Mother and Child stand beneath a canopy, and a candle burns continually before the statue, an acknowledgement of the petitions placed before the Virgin.

On the feast of the Assumption in 1937 the restored shrine with the statue of Our Lady was dedicated in the presence of a crowd of 4,000 people who joined in the procession.

Although the divisions and strife of four centuries dictated that the shrine could not return to its original home in what had become the Anglican church, it was noted at the time that the vicar of St Gregory's church altered the time of evensong to allow the Catholics who were organizing the procession to direct the crowds across the Croft to the church of Our Lady and St John beside the Anglican church.

The annual procession, which was known in pre-Reformation days as 'Our Lady of the Harvest', is now known locally as 'Our Lady's Homecoming'. It takes place on the Sunday closest to the feast of the Assumption and in past years the statue has been taken on the Saturday evening to rest overnight at the nearby convent.

Pilgrims come from all over East Anglia to join the Catholic parishioners of Our Lady and St John the Evangelist, many of them carrying sheaves of corn as Sudbury pilgrims would have carried them before the Reformation. Hymns are sung and the rosary is recited. When the procession reaches the Catholic church, the Magnificat is sung. The statue is placed on a small altar in the attractive garden where a finely carved set of the Mysteries of the Rosary is to be seen. The final event of the day is a party and barbecue. At 10.00pm the statue is carried from the garden into the church and the day ends with the singing of Compline, a memorable occasion to which visitors are warmly welcomed.

In 2002 for the first time the statue of Our Lady was invited to rest, on the Saturday night before the procession, in the chapel of Our Lady and St Anne in the Church of St Gregory, her original home in Sudbury. It was a moving homecoming, the culmination of many years of friendship, prayer and co-operation between the two Christian communities which must surely pave the way to the restoration of shared devotion to Our Lady in this fascinating place.

Shrine – Sudbury

LOCATION/ DIRECTIONS	From the M25, exit J28 Take the A12 towards Chelmsford A131 to Braintree/Sudbury Church of Our Lady and St John can be found off Gregory Street behind St Gregory's Church on the Croft alongside the River Stour BY RAIL From London Liverpool Street to Sudbury, approx. 1hr 20min
CONTACT TEL. NUMBERS	Our Lady and St John the Evangelist 20 The Croft Sudbury Suffolk CO10 1HW Tel. 01787 372703
EMAIL ADDRESS	ourlady@stjohntheevangelist.fsnet.co.uk
WEB SITE	www.ourladyofsudbury.co.uk
TIMES OF SERVICES	Monthly day of recollection: 1st Saturday of the month, 10.30am–4.00pm Shrine Prayers: every Saturday 10.30am Saturday Mass: 5.00pm for Sunday Sunday Mass: 9.30am
SPECIAL DATES/ EVENTS/ FESTIVALS/ PILGRIMAGES	Sunday after Assumption – Homecoming of Our Lady at sundown
ANGLICAN CHURCH AND CONTACT TEL. NUMBERS	St Gregory The Rectory Christopher Lane Sudbury Tel. 01787 372611

LOCAL ATTRACTIONS	Sudbury • Gainsborough House – home of Thomas Gainsborough and museum • River walks along the Stour. 3 miles away the historical village of Long Melford www.longmelford.co.uk take the A134 towards Bury St Edmunds • Melford Hall, National Trust • Holy Trinity Church • Antique Shops ('Lovejoy' TV series filmed here!)
GOOD PUBS	Wagon and Horses The Mill Hotel
PLACES FOR PILGRIMS TO STAY	Contact Tourist Information Town Hall Market Hall Sudbury Tel. 01787 881320

21

Tower Hill

OUR LADY OF GRACES
TOWER HILL

As an island race and a seafaring nation, many of our stories and
legends are woven around the dangers faced by sailors and their
reliance upon the powers of heaven to ensure their safety. The
London shrine of St Mary Graces at Tower Hill is one of a number
of English shrines whose origins lie in tales of the sea.

The present shrine in the church of the English Martyrs at Tower Hill commemorates the Cistercian abbey of St Mary Graces which now lies beneath the Royal Mint building. On either side of the altar are large mosaics illustrating the dramatic events that led to the founding of the abbey. The first picture shows the imminent shipwreck of King Edward III in the fourteenth century. In the second, calm has been restored and the King is inviting the Cisterican monks of Beaulieu Abbey in Hampshire to take possession of his new abbey which he has dedicated to St Mary Graces in thanksgiving for his safe deliverance. In the background the Tower of London is a foreboding presence.

In 1538 the abbey of St Mary Graces was suppressed and the grounds converted into gardens. During the reign of Queen Elizabeth, the area became the naval victualling yard, and was subsequently referred to by Samuel Pepys writing in the reign of Charles II. For another two hundred years the few remaining Catholics of Tower Hill had to fend for themselves.

Gradually the area fell into decay and poverty, bringing in its wake the squalor of slums whose notoriety became the backdrop for several of the novels of Charles Dickens. The proximity of the docks on the River Thames made the area a haven for immigrants in the aftermath of the Napoleonic Wars. In 1846 the repeal of the Corn Laws brought thousands of agricultural workers to the city in search of work. The resulting unemployment and lack of sanitation brought untold suffering, but little or nothing was done to improve matters.

While on a visit to England in 1864, the founder of the Oblates of Mary Immaculate, Blessed Eugene de Mazenod, visited Tower Hill and saw for himself the misery and poverty. The Order had been founded in France to care for the poor, and little time was wasted in setting up a mission in the London area. In 1864 the opening of the Tower Hill Mission was announced, and local Catholics gathered beneath the railway arch on Tower Hill for the first celebration of Mass in three hundred years. From that day to the present, the Mission has been in the care of the Oblate Fathers.

The devoted care given by the priests and nuns of the Mission to the nineteenth-century inhabitants of Tower Hill is legendary. In 1867 they were called upon to deal with a severe outbreak of cholera. This disaster finally brought the plight of the people of the area to the attention of the civil authorities, and long-overdue slum clearance was at last under way.

During the early years of the twentieth century, the clearance continued. In the Second World War severe bombing wrought further profound changes, and the area is now altered beyond recognition. The church of the English Martyrs appears to be dwarfed by the prosperity of the City of London spilling out into the neighbourhood. The pale brick and stone church is encircled by roads clogged with traffic and surrounded by towering banks and insurance buildings. It stands alone in a sea of steel and glass, the neighbouring presbytery sheltered behind protective iron railings.

On the day of my visit, the parish priest opened the door to me, but conversation was impossible above the roar of traffic. We passed into the presbytery before entering the church itself. Silence descended and a fine interior designed by Pugin was revealed. Father Malachy Lynch led the way to the shrine of Our Lady of Grace, as it is known.

The shrine in the north transept forms a separate chapel framed in a slender arch. The imposing statue of Our Lady of Graces is carved in Carrara marble. She stands surrounded by alabaster angels and bathed in the light that shines through a concealed window overhead. The small altar in front of the statue is decorated with lilies entwined with ribbons bearing the words '*Ave Maria Gratia Plena*'. Kneeling on guard above the tabernacle are two angels carved in white marble.

This shrine commemorates the abbey of Our Lady of Grace which stood here four and a half centuries ago. The close proximity of the Tower of London is a bleak reminder of the tragedies of the sixteenth century when brave men and women died for their faith. One of Our Lady's titles is Queen of Martyrs, and the armorial bearings of ten of the martyrs are attached to the iron grille beside the high altar which is dedicated to the English Martyrs.

This fine church also recalls more recent events. A day in 1935 lingers in the memory of older parishioners: the day when a procession was organized by the Guild of Our Lady of Ransom to honour the canonization of St John Fisher and St Thomas More. The procession attracted thousands of Catholics, many of whom had travelled great distances to be present along the route from Lincoln's Inn Fields to the site of the scaffold on which both martyrs had been beheaded.

The Tower

I decided to return to explore this connection with the Tower of London and to find the burial places of these two English saints, whose memorials stand beside Our Lady's shrine.

Emerging from the jostling crowds at Tower Hill underground station the following day, I came upon a vast sundial, beneath which the history of the area is illustrated on a circular brass plaque. Although the span of time allotted to this story stretches from the year 910 to the present day, no mention is made of the Reformation and of the many executions which took place only feet away from this spot. The history of Tower Hill is marked with heroic convictions and terrible deeds, but this goes unremarked on the base of the sundial.

The site of the scaffold is surrounded by palm trees, and in the centre are stones inscribed with the names of those who died here. The whole is contained in a garden which was closed on the day of my visit; tall metal fencing separated garden and shrine from the strutting pigeons and the crowds who wander by unaware, for the most part, of the tragedy that still lingers in the summer air.

Those who were martyred were not always possessed of heroic courage. With notable exceptions, they were ordinary people who had never expected to be asked to deny everything that they held most dear: the very map of their existence and their path to heaven. Their beliefs were betrayed by those in whom they had placed their trust.

Having refused to acknowledge the justice of their cause, the King turned to more pleasant pastimes. Some of the martyrs languished in prison and were eventually executed on Tower Hill. Others were abandoned to the whim of torturers, whose cruelty knew no bounds, before being dragged to Tyburn where they died a pitiful death.

In the heart of William the Conqueror's great fortress lies the Beauchamp Tower, which houses the list of those who died here for their faith. At the top of its narrow winding stairs is the cell in which St Philip Howard spent the last eleven years of his life.

In a cool and shadowy crypt beneath the royal chapel of St Peter ad Vincula there lies the body of St Thomas More. The kindly guide who ushered me down the stone steps remarked conversationally that Sir Thomas' head was not here; it lies in the Roper Vault at St Dunstain's Church in Canterbury, with the remains of his beloved daughter Margaret.

Few of those who throng the Tower from across the world have any reason to appreciate the tragedies that were played out within these walls. The atmosphere is nevertheless one of restraint.

I walk out through the gate of the Tower, past the rows of coaches beside the ubiquitous McDonald's. A lone speaker is inveighing against some unfathomable wrong, but his words are drowned by the roar of traffic and so I pass him by. A few steps away stands the city church of All Hallows by the Tower where the heroic Bishop of Rochester, St John Fisher, was buried in 1535. This fine church was bombed in 1941 but rose phoenix-like from the ashes and was rededicated in 1957. It is a precious place of prayer for those who live and work in the city of London.

The history of the church is well documented. Originally there stood to the north of the present day church a chapel, dedicated to the Blessed Virgin, which was built by Richard Coeur de Lion and endowed by the abbess of nearby Barking. Edward I later appointed it to be a chantry, and an offering was made in 1503 by King Henry VII to the miraculous statue of Our Lady, which St Thomas More described as 'looking down on the fishwives of Billingsgate'.

TOWER HILL

I returned to the shrine of Our Lady of Graces within the nearby church of the English Martyrs in time for the daily Mass. Prayer is continuous in this beautiful building, and it is easy to imagine the approval of John Fisher and Thomas More at the revival of the shrine of Our Lady of Graces under the watchful eye of Our Lady, Queen of Martyrs.

Shrine – Our Lady of Grace – Tower Hill

LOCATION/ DIRECTIONS	London Underground, District Line Tower Hill Station Walk towards Tower Gateway Station (DLR) turn left into Minories turn right into Goodmans Yard cross over at traffic lights into Prescot Street the Church of the English Martys is on the right- hand side
CONTACT TEL. NUMBERS	30 Prescot Street London E1 8BB Tel. 020 7488 4654
EMAIL ADDRESS	martyrstowerhill@btinternet.com
TIMES OF SERVICES	Sunday Masses Saturday vigil at 6.30pm, Sunday 9.00am and 11.00am Weekday Masses Tuesday to Friday Mass at 1pm Holy Day Masses Vigil eve of feast 6.30pm Feast Day 9.30am, 12 noon and 1.00pm
ANGLICAN CHURCH AND CONTACT TEL. NUMBERS	St Olave (signposted from Tower Hill Tube) 8 Hart Street London Tel. 020 7488 4318 Burial place of Samuel Pepys and his wife Elizabeth Crypt Chapel 13th c. Church Tower 15th c. Lunchtime recitals, most Wednesdays and Thursdays 1st and 3rd Sunday, Eucharist at 11am Thursdays at 8.30am
LOCAL ATTRACTIONS	Tower of London Old Royal Mint Trinity House
GOOD PUBS	Many bars and restaurants in the area

22

Truro

TRURO

The Shrine of Our Lady of the Portal

The Catholic church of Our Lady of the Portal and St Piran is close to a large roundabout and surrounded by dual carriageways. At first sight it would be hard to guess that devotion to Our Lady of the Portal has a fascinating history which connects this shrine with early Rome, the holy mountain of Athos and Moscow's Kremlin. There is also an association with the Old Pretender, James Edward Stuart, and his son Henry, the Cardinal Duke of York.

The Cornish capital of Truro is a bustling city with a small harbour. In medieval times the shrine to Our Lady of the Portal – Our Lady of the Gateway – stood at the main entrance to the town, where it flourished until the Dissolution. No one knows exactly when the shrine was founded and it probably stretches back to the years following the Norman Conquest. Now, at the start of the third millennium, the shrine of Our Lady of the Portal is restored and a fine statue stands in the modern church.

In medieval times the guilds of Truro included that of 'Mary Portell' which cared for the well-being, both spiritual and temporal, of its members. Amongst their works of charity the guilds enabled pilgrims to visit shrines; they also mended highways and built bridges; the guild of Mary Portell may thus have been responsible for the bridge across the Truro River at the entrance to the town and for its small chapel. In many towns bridges were built with sanctuaries combining practicality with devotion, for the need to cross the water in safety was filled with spiritual association.

A priest who served as chaplain to the guild would base himself at the chapel on the bridge and devote his time to the care of visitors. The departing traveller would be sent on his way with a prayer for his safety and the reminder that life itself is a journey. Those coming and going would place their life in the hands of Our Lady, reciting the Greek Orthodox refrain 'Hail Blessed Lady of the Portal, opening the gate of Paradise to the faithful'.

The shrine in Truro was predated by some six hundred years by the Madonna del Portico in Rome, although perhaps down the centuries word of this had reached the people of Truro from the merchants who sailed into port with their Roman cargo. The port of Truro was indeed a significant point of access for merchants from many parts of Europe.

The origins of the name 'Our Lady of the Portal' are to be found in Rome where the fifth-century Roman Christian, Galla, received an icon of the Blessed Virgin from two angels. After her death, her house became known as the Oratorio di Santa Galla. Since the Oratorio was situated near the Portico d'Ottavia, the Gate of Octavius, the icon became known as the Madonna del Portico – Our Lady of the Gate. In the sixth century it was carried through Rome in procession by Pope John I during a time of plague, and many miracles were recorded.

The little Oratorio was eventually demolished, and in its place the present church of Santa Maria in Campitelli was built in 1659, and continued to house the Madonna del Portico. It was a centre of great devotion, and eighteenth-century visitors to the shrine included the Old Pretender, James Edward Stuart, son of King James II. James Edward finished his days in Rome where he prayed continually before the icon of the Madonna del Portico for the return of the Catholic faith to England. His prayer is still echoed in the Church of Santa Maria in Campitelli, and Saturday devotions to the Madonna del Portico include prayer for the return of England to her ancient faith. His son Henry, Cardinal Duke of York, wrote a paper in which he made reference to the legends of various icons of Our Lady of the Portal.

Another icon of Our Lady of the Portal is to be found on Mount Athos and is said to be miraculous. Its history goes back to the ninth century when a poor woman of Nicaea outside Constantinople possessed a miraculous icon which became the object of iconoclastic fury. A soldier struck the face of the Blessed Virgin and blood was seen to flow from the wound. He immediately repented and decided to enter a monastery. Before doing so he advised the woman to cast the icon on the sea in order to save

it from destruction. To her great surprise and joy, the icon did not sink but floated away upright on the waves.

Legend has it that it reappeared some two centuries later on the waters surrounding Mount Athos from whence it was rescued by the monks of the Iveron monastery. Wishing to protect the icon, the monks placed it within their own monastery, but each evening it vanished, only to be found the following morning beside their gateway. Perplexed by this strange happening, the monks continued to retrieve the icon each morning and bring it back inside the monastery. It eventually became clear to them that Our Lady was trying to tell them that she did not wish the monks to care for her. It was rather her desire to care for them. The icon was therefore

OUR LADY OF THE PORTAL
TRURO

installed in a small sanctuary by the gate and named the Portaitissa. The mark of the blow delivered by the ninth-century soldier is still visible. There is a tradition on Mount Athos that, should this icon and two others vanish from the mountain, the community on Mount Athos will also disappear.

In the seventeenth century, a copy of the Portaitissa was taken to Russia by Patriarch Nikon and installed in the Kremlin in Moscow. It was named the Iverskaya and became one of the most beloved of all the great Moscow icons. It remained in the Kremlin, the source of many blessings, until the Revolution of 1917 when it disappeared. A copy was smuggled out of Russia and found its way to the Anglican shrine of Our Lady at Walsingham, where for a time a lamp was maintained before it by the revived Fraternity of Our Lady of the Portal. There are still hopes that the original icon may have remained in Moscow.

Our Lady of the Portal

In 1965 the Fraternity of Our Lady of the Portal was reinstated in Truro by Father Wilfrid Wharton, and Dr Margaret Pollard, who dedicated her life to restoring both this shrine and Ladye Park in Liskeard. The membership is world-wide, and money was sought and raised in order to build a new church and restore the ancient shrine. There was some difficulty in deciding the site for the new church, until a previously unknown spring was discovered in an overgrown garden on land belonging to the Fraternity. It was immediately decided that this was a perfect site for the proposed church of Our Lady of the Portal and St Piran, the sixth-century Cornish saint. A plaque in the church marks the site of the spring beneath.

The design is partly Byzantine with a porch or narthex running the width of the building. On either side of the altar are paintings by the Norwegian artist, Lars Prag; on the left is a Russian icon of Our Lady's Annunciation, and on the right the 'Old Testament Trinity'. A section of the narthex is separated from the rest of the building by wrought-iron gates that lead into the shrine.

The statue of Our Lady nursing her Child is 350 years old and comes from the Basque region of the Pyrenees. At its foot are twelve tapestry kneelers sewn by members of the Fraternity of Our Lady of the Portal, each one featuring a different flower associated with the Blessed Virgin, with words from the Litany of Loretto stitched beneath. A silver lamp by Dunstan Pruden which hangs in the shrine is the gift of two Cornish widows in honour of the widowhood of Our Lady, and in prayer for the widows of the world. The stained-glass windows are the work of the Benedictine monk Charles Norris of Buckfast; they fill the shrine with blue light in the morning, and in the evening this changes to yellow and orange as the sun moves round.

Pope Saint Pius X added the title 'Our Lady of All Christians' to the image of Our Lady of the Portal. This designation is reflected in the ecumenical work of Truro through which the prayer life of this holy place is being renewed. Amid the traffic and bustle of the twenty-first century, Our Lady of the Portal has returned to Cornwall.

Shrine – Truro

LOCATION/ DIRECTIONS	From M25 Exit J15, M4 West M5 South A30 Bodmin/Redruth A39/A390 Truro At the large roundabout by Police Station turn into St Austell Street
CONTACT TEL. NUMBERS	Our Lady of the Portal and St Piran St Austell Street Truro Cornwall TR1 1SE Tel. 01872 272291
EMAIL ADDRESS	stpiran@btinternet.com
WEB SITE	www.plymouth-diocese.org.uk/parishes/cornwall/truro.htm
TIMES OF SERVICES	MASS Saturday (for Sunday) 7pm Sundays 9.30am and 11am Daily 9.30am Wednesday 10.00am Thursday 7.15pm Sacrament of Reconciliation, Saturday after mass and 6–6.30pm
SPECIAL DATES/ EVENTS/ FESTIVALS/ PILGRIMAGES	Pilgrimages by arrangement
ROSARY GROUP	Meet after Mass most mornings
ANGLICAN CHURCH AND CONTACT TEL. NUMBERS	Truro Cathedral 14 St Mary's Street Truro Tel. 01872 276782 www.truro.anglican.org

LOCAL ATTRACTIONS	Historic city centre of Truro
	Eden Project within 10 mile radius
GOOD PUBS	Many pubs, cafés and restaurants in city centre
PLACES FOR PILGRIMS TO STAY	Contact Tourist Information Centre Tel. 01872 322900 www.cornwalltouristboard.co.uk

23

Walsingham

More books have been written, more poems recited and more songs sung about Walsingham than about any other shrine in England. In the medieval world, this place of pilgrimage ranked fourth after Jerusalem, Compostela and Rome, and it was the only one of the four to be dedicated specifically to the Blessed Virgin. The history of this place stretches back to the eleventh century, and today Walsingham is once again the leading shrine dedicated to Our Lady in England, the focus of her dowry and the designated National Shrine.

The village of Little Walsingham lies deep in the East Anglian countryside. Despite the comings and goings of the thousands of pilgrims who travel here from around the globe, the fields and woodland that surround this little Norfolk village remain unchanged. Farmers continue to cultivate their land, and sheep graze in the shadow of the ancient ruins, unperturbed by the passing pilgrims.

There are several famous medieval pilgrimage routes to Walsingham starting from Canterbury, London or further afield, and there are less notable but well-trodden lanes leading across the hills in the surrounding countryside. In the irresistibly-named village of Great Snoring, a local inhabitant pointed out a path leading across the village green. I set off along one of the many pilgrim ways, alongside fields of spring corn, the way lined with cowslips and violets. I passed through woods of oak, eventually descending to a lane leading to the Slipper Chapel.

With moorhen, duck and stately swan for company, I followed the lane along the river to the chapel, which stands a mile from the ruins of the great priory. As I walked, I thought of those kings and queens who came to Walsingham: of the de Clares who first endowed the sanctuary and its possessions, and of the many great names that appear in the story of this corner of Our Lady's Dowry.

It is tempting to dwell on the history of Walsingham, but this can lead to a nostalgia that overlooks the importance of all that is happening here today. As if to underline such thoughts, and in contrast to the peace, huge coaches swished past me, filled with pilgrims from all over the world, and I stepped aside on to the river bank and watched them pass by.

The Slipper Chapel is now the Catholic Shrine of Our Lady of Walsingham; it stands beside the more recent chapel of Our Lady of Reconciliation, a Norfolk barn design that merges comfortably into the surrounding countryside. The Slipper Chapel is not dwarfed by its magnificent new neighbour, but sits neatly apart surrounded by box-edged gardens filled with lavender and roses.

As I sit drawing, people pass to and fro, peacefully wandering from bookshop to tea room but always drawn back to the shrine of Our Lady in the Slipper Chapel as if unable to tear themselves away.

One lady pauses to tell me that this is her twenty-fifth annual visit to Walsingham. She explains that her husband drives coaches and brings a pilgrimage each year and she joins him. As we talk, she radiates affection for the place. Every journey here is eagerly anticipated, as they long to revisit Mary who is their close friend,

to tell her their news, good and bad, and to receive her blessing
and the assurance of her prayer. There is an implicit loyalty to
Walsingham in her manner, and when I mention other shrines her
glance tells me quite clearly that I have been fickle. This is the
high note of the year for this couple. In the summer, she tells me,
the fields beside the shrine are filled with tents and caravans as vast
numbers of young people come to renew their Christian faith.

More coaches arrive, and there is an air of expectant activity as
the time for the daily Mass approaches. People quietly wend their
way towards the church and the courtyard is empty once more.

In the new-found silence in the garden around me, the history of
this little chapel fills the air. Silence is never absolute in the
country; there is always the sound of birds, the distant crow of a
cockerel, and around the lavender by Our Lady's chapel there is
the hum of bees. It must have been thus long ago when the earliest pilgrims arrived in Walsingham, tired after their long journey
following the roadside shrines and crosses that marked the
'Walsingham Way' to visit England's Nazareth. Those who travelled across the sea, landed at King's Lynn nearby.

This was the last stopping-place the pilgrims reached before their
final goal in Walsingham. The chapel was built in the fourteenth
century, and was originally named after St Catherine of
Alexandria, patroness of pilgrims. Many of the pilgrims wished to
walk barefoot for the last mile which led them to the shrine of Our

Lady beside the great priory in Walsingham village. One legend suggests that this was the origin of the name 'Slipper Chapel'. They left their shoes at the chapel in safe keeping and it soon became known as 'the Slipper Chapel'.

The statue of Our Lady of Walsingham in the chapel is a copy of the fifteenth-century seal of Walsingham priory. Mary wears a Saxon crown, a symbol of her ancient queenship, as she reaches out in motherhood to all and presents her Son to the world. At the time of the Dissolution of the monasteries, the original statue was seized, taken to London and burnt. In 1982 the new statue was taken to London for a very different purpose. Its destination was Wembley Stadium, where it was placed upon the altar at which Pope John Paul II celebrated Mass.

At the back of the Slipper Chapel, a stained-glass window represents the Annunciation. It was installed in 1997, a gift of the Guild of Our Lady of Ransom and designed by the artist, Arthur Fisher. The subject of the picture perpetuates the affection in which this feast is held in East Anglia, and many of the windows of the village churches depict the appearance of the Angel Gabriel to Mary.

Until the mid-sixteenth century, the angelus bell was a familiar sound as it rang out across the fields to announce the time of prayer to Our Lady at dawn, at noon and at sunset.

As Mass ends, the crowds spill out across the paths and lawn, eager for food and relaxation. I pack my drawing things away and set off along the Holy Mile from the Slipper Chapel to Walsingham village. I pass others walking the same path and there is a shared warmth of friendship: all thoughts of daily routine are banished in the joy of pilgrimage through this glorious countryside.

In the village, an almost continental atmosphere greets the visitor. Shops display statues and holy objects, happily juxtaposed with the newspapers of the day and pots of honey from the Walsingham apiary. Behind a wall and through the trees I can see the ruins of the great arch of the east window of the ancient Augustinian priory.

In the village square, 'Common Place', a small museum beside the entrance to the priory ruins gives an illustrated history of the Walsingham Shrine. In 1852 the priory passed into the hands of the Rev. Daniel Lee Warner and, with his nephew the Rev. James Lee Warner, he set about excavating the site. The museum display includes sepia grained photographs of soberly-clad archaeologists in dark suits and bowler hats, standing frozen in time before the revealed foundations of the priory church. Leaving these displays, the doorway opens on to a path which circles the lawns of the abbey precincts.

All that remains of the priory today is the lofty eastern gable some seventy feet high, flanked by staircases and turrets, and across the lawns there are two ponds. Close by, a small stone marks the spot where England's little House of Nazareth once stood, the shrine in honour of Our Lady of Walsingham.

WALSINGHAM

The present owners, relations of the Lee Warners and descendants of the family into whose hands the priory grounds passed in 1660, have allowed time to deal gently with the ruins. Too many places fall victim to the whims of heritage committees and lose their fragile but essential characteristics. At Walsingham the lawns stretch down to the river, and the ruins stand undisturbed.

Walsingham Abbey is a post-Reformation private house built in the grounds of the priory. It stands beside part of the original cloister and cellar. The birds sing, and the air seems peopled with the saints who were always here; only the mortal remains of their buildings have fallen away.

The Holy House

Towards the end of the reign of Edward the Confessor and only five years before the Norman invasion of 1066, Richeldis de

Faverches, the lady of the manor of Walsingham, had a dream. In her dream, the Blessed Virgin transported her to the Holy House of Nazareth and, while Richeldis gazed at the home of the Holy Family, Our Lady requested that one of its like should be built in Walsingham. The dream was repeated three times, and Richeldis did her best to carry out Our Lady's wish.

Try as they might, her builders were defeated. Richeldis retired to her room to pray throughout the night. As morning came, she saw to her delight that the house had been built by the angels, not in the place she had chosen, but some two hundred feet away, in the place where Our Lady wished it to be. In this place, Mary had explained, the people would celebrate the Annunciation, the 'root of man's gracious redemption'. She also delivered a promise to future generations who might visit Walsingham: 'Whosoever seeks my help here will not go away empty-handed'. The little shrine was to become a place of prayer and consolation for people from all corners of the world.

Pilgrimage was a way of life for people of the eleventh and twelfth centuries. The events recounted in the legend of Richeldis took place just before the age of the Crusades when it became extremely hazardous to journey to the holy places of Jerusalem. Word spread concerning England's own Holy House of Nazareth deep in the East Anglian countryside, and pilgrims wasted no time in turning towards this heaven-sent alternative.

Richeldis' only son, Geoffrey de Faverches decided to establish a foundation to care for his mother's sanctuary. Its fame had spread and pilgrims were coming in ever-increasing numbers. A great priory was built beside the little house of Nazareth and sometime between 1130 and 1153 it passed into the care of the Augustinian canons. Eventually even greater protection was needed for the fragile wattle and daub walls of the Holy House, and a chapel of stone was constructed to enclose them.

Records are filled with the names of the rich and famous who travelled here. In an age that was harsh and dangerous and in which life expectancy was short, most people were only too aware of the contrariness of fate. Prayer and dedication to their especial saints raised all men to equality. With the kings and queens came their subjects, for pilgrimage was a merry as well as an improving pastime and the crowds that thronged to Walsingham have been described as the football crowds of their day. These people shared a profound belief in the power of prayer, and the journey of pilgrimage was a reflection of the journey of life, a quest for a treasure that lay beyond this world.

Henry II was one of the first kings to come to Walsingham, probably in penance for his part in the murder in 1170 of his Archbishop of Canterbury, Thomas à Becket, which so outraged Europe that the King spent the rest of his life seeking forgiveness. It is said that he visited the shrine of Our Lady of Walsingham no less than nine times, and left 3,000 tapers to light it.

In 1383 King Richard II came to Walsingham; he was the boy king who stood bravely before his poverty-stricken people in an attempt to restore peace at the time of the Peasants' Revolt in 1381. Before setting out for Smithfield to meet the insurgents, he prayed at the great shrine of St Edward the Confessor in Westminster Abbey. It is conjectured that he also prayed at the neighbouring shrine of Our Lady of Pew. Richard subsequently returned to the abbey to give thanks for the intercession of Our Lady, and it was at this time that England was acknowledged as the Dowry of Mary.

In July 1498 Margaret Beaufort, Countess of Richmond and Derby, embarked on a tour of Our Lady's shrines in East Anglia with her son, King Henry VII. Before leaving Windsor, the King's mother stopped to order brooches for her grandchildren from a local gold-smith. It was perhaps on this occasion that she ordered the silver-gilt statue of her son which Henry bequeathed in his will to the shrine of Our Lady of Walsingham. Such was the heat in that July of 1498 that, as the party travelled from the shrine of Our Lady in the great abbey of Thetford, the King's mother abandoned her carriage and was carried by servants on a litter, stopping repeatedly for cool drinks.

Indirectly, Lady Margaret was responsible for the dramatic increase in the publicity received by the shrine at the end of the fifteenth century. In her employ was a young printer named Richard Pynson who had set up his own printing press in succession to the first English printer, William Caxton.

In 1490 Pynson became the chief printer of law books in London. He also published many prayer books and translations of pious works for the countess. His work includes a lengthy poem by an unidentified author, which became known as the 'Pynson Ballad', and tells the story of Richeldis and the little House of Nazareth at Walsingham.

> O England great cause thou hast glad for to be
> Compared to the land of promise Sion
> Thou attainest by grace to stand in that degree
> Through this glorious Lady's supportation
> To be called in every realm and region

The Holy Land Our Lady's Dowry
Thus art thou named of old antiquity.

And this is the cause as it appeareth by likliness
In thee is builded new Nazareth a mansion
To the honour of the heavenly empress
And of her most glorious salutation
When Gabriel said at old Nazareth ave
This joy here daily remembered for to be.

The ballad was written in English, and for this reason it reached the ears of many who were still unfamiliar with the story of Walsingham.

In the early years of the sixteenth century, the Dutch scholar Erasmus visited Walsingham and sent a description to King Henry VIII; 'You will say that it is the seat of the Gods, so bright and shining as it is all over with jewels, gold and silver'.

Henry VIII came to Walsingham for the first time in 1511 in gratitude for the birth of his shortlived son, Prince Henry. On this occasion he walked barefoot from East Barsham Manor, some two miles distant, and left a valuable necklace for the Virgin's statue. There can have been little cause for concern about the future of Walsingham. Neither would there have been any intimation of what lay ahead. It is a sad footnote that on his deathbed King Henry VIII was heard praying to Our Lady of Walsingham.

Less than thirty years after the King's visit, and upon his order, the shrine and the priory were closed. The statue of Mary was taken to Chelsea and burned in the presence of Thomas Cromwell. The prior of Walsingham and most of the members of his community were amongst the first to sign the Oath of Supremacy. The sub-prior Nicholas Mileham was charged with conspiring to rebel against the suppression of the lesser monasteries. He was hanged outside the priory walls with a layman, George Gysborough.

Standing in the gardens of Walsingham Abbey among the priory ruins, one can picture the desolation that followed. The memory of the singing and chanting of the monks faded; the figures of the pilgrims became a distant memory; echoes of their footsteps and the hoofbeats of the King's horses ringing on the stones faded into silence.

In the years that followed the priory was abandoned, and the pilgrims' way reverted to a tangled wilderness of flowers choked with weeds and encroaching woodland. It is said that in 1578 St

Philip Howard, Earl of Arundel, visited Walsingham in the company of Queen Elizabeth, and left a haunting lament.

> Owls do screech where sweetest hymns
> Lately were sung,
> Toads and serpents hold their dens
> Where the pilgrims did throng.
>
> Weep weep O Walsingham
> Whose days are nights,
> Blessings turned to blasphemies,
> Holy deeds to despites.
>
> Sin is where Our Lady sat,
> Heaven turned to hell;
> Satan sits where Our Lord held sway,
> Walsingham O farewell.

In 1585 Philip Howard became a Catholic and was imprisoned in the Tower of London, where he died in 1595.

For nearly three hundred and fifty years the village of Walsingham retreated into anonymity. The priory fell into greater ruin, a ghostly memory in the grounds of the post-Reformation Walsingham Abbey.

The Slipper Chapel had escaped destruction, but instead became a farm building. During the next three centuries, stories were told of Catholics who sought permission from the farmer to enter his barn, there to say a prayer to the Lady of Walsingham.

Then came remarkable stirrings of a new beginning and the restoration of this great centre of pilgrimage was at last under way. Charlotte Pearson Boyd had become interested in the Slipper Chapel during the 1860s, when she noticed a building outside Walsingham which was being used as a barn but appeared to be a medieval chapel. Miss Boyd was a devout Anglican, greatly interested in assisting newly-formed Anglican religious orders. She determined that the medieval Slipper Chapel should be restored to religious use. In the 1890s she was able to purchase the building from the Lee Warner family, and began extensive restoration work. Before it was completed, Miss Boyd became a Roman Catholic. After the restoration was completed she confided the building to the Benedictines of Downside Abbey, who subsequently passed it on to the local Roman Catholic bishop.

Miss Boyd was determined that the Slipper Chapel should

become the home of Our Lady's shrine although the Catholic hierarchy initially showed little interest in her plan. The shrine of Our Lady of Walsingham had recently been established in nearby King's Lynn, and it was generally recognized that there was little likelihood of any restoration of the priory of Walsingham.

Miss Boyd persevered, but it was not until 1934 that her dream at last became a reality – long after her death in 1906. In 1934 the National Shrine of Our Lady of Walsingham was established at the Slipper Chapel, and King's Lynn relinquished its claim. In that year Cardinal Bourne, Archbishop of Westminster, led the first national pilgrimage in four hundred years and the Slipper Chapel was named the National Shrine. The little building had been skilfully restored, and in 1938 a chapel dedicated to the Holy Ghost, a sacristy and a short cloister were added.

The first Mass to be celebrated in the grounds of the priory since the Dissolution took place in 1945, organized by United States servicemen stationed in Norfolk. Today a shrine to Our Lady of Walsingham stands in Williamsburg, Virginia.

To accommodate the vast numbers, the barn-like chapel of Our Lady of Reconciliation now stands beside the ancient Slipper Chapel. It is all that is practical and quotidian – our daily bread of life and prayer. In the courtyard that divides the two starkly different buildings, fourteen crosses form the Way of the Cross; each one was carried here by groups travelling from different corners of the British Isles in reparation for the ravages of the Second World War.

Modern Walsingham

In a description of the original shrine, the nineteenth-century antiquary Henry Harrod observed: 'Almost from the foundation of the Priory up to the dissolution, there was one unceasing movement of pilgrims to and from Walsingham'; the scene is once more one of continual pilgrimage throughout the year.

Clustered around this place of unearthly silence there are now six chapels of different denominations: two Anglican, two Catholic, one Methodist, and a small Orthodox chapel, with its golden dome shining incongruously in the Norfolk sunshine.

In the 1920s the restored Slipper Chapel was little used. Meanwhile, under the guidance of Father Alfred Hope Patten, a new Anglican church and shrine was built in the heart of Walsingham village. He arranged that a new statue of the Blessed Virgin should be carved from the ancient priory seal. The statue was originally placed in the parish church of St Mary. On 15

October 1931, the feast of St Teresa of Avila, the statue was translated to a new Holy House built within a small church which was enlarged to form the Anglican shrine as it is today.

Surrounding the main altar of the church, fifteen chapels with finely decorated altars and screens depict the fifteen mysteries of the rosary, each chapel peopled with figures of the saints. This church is the guardian of ancient prayers that give meaning to the essential Englishness of Our Lady's Dowry. Pilgrimages take place with increasing frequency, and the rosary is recited every evening in this beautiful church.

The church is reached along Knight's Street, close to Knight's Gate on the northern boundary of the walls of Walsingham Abbey. Both take their name from the legend of the fourteenth-century Sir Ralph Boutetourt, who, in the year 1314, found himself outside the gates of the priory with an enemy in hot pursuit. The gate was bolted and, to the sound of rapidly approaching hoofs, Sir Ralph implored Our Lady to hear his prayer for sanctuary. In an instant the astonished Sir Ralph found himself within the gates.

And finally, the Orthodox Chapel of St Seraphim, so ordinary in

external appearance – there is little need to explain that it was once the railway station. Since the 1960s it has been used as a church for the Orthodox community.

On entering this strange building, time is needed for one's eyes to become accustomed to the darkness. Gradually in the candlelight the almond eyes of the saints, glowing from the icons, penetrate the gloom. The description of Erasmus, when writing in 1511 to Henry VIII about the Holy House at the beginning of the sixteenth century, comes to mind: 'There is a small chapel, which admits by a small narrow little door, on either side, those who come to salute our Ladye; the light is feeble, in fact scarcely any, excepting from wax candles. A most delightful fragrance gladdens one's nose.'

That building too had its shortcomings, for in the same year Erasmus wrote; 'The place is very draughty on all sides; the windows are open, and the doors are open, and not far off is the ocean, the father of the winds.' In response, Henry sent twenty pounds to pay for the services of a glazier. The numinous atmosphere of the pre-Reformation Holy House drew kings and queens with their multitude of followers, and this small Orthodox chapel with a silent, palpable sanctity prompts the spirit to lift in recognition of its wonder.

Walsingham is once more the main centre of pilgrimage in England, and yet it retains the atmosphere of a Norfolk village in its gentle surroundings and intimate lanes. The shrine of Our Lady speaks to us of the intimacy and sanctity of family life, and also of the motherhood of Mary which extends to all humanity. In the silence of her shrine, the needs of the poor, the lonely and the persecuted are lovingly and compassionately welcomed by the Mother who brings a message of joy and hope to a troubled world.

Shrine – Walsingham

LOCATION/ DIRECTIONS	From M25, exit J27 M11, exit J9 and A11 to Barton Hills A1065 to Fakenham. B1105 towards Wells-next-the-Sea; after a short distance follow the signs for Little Walsingham – Light Vehicles Only, which takes you through the villages of East Barsham and Houghton St Giles. The Shrine is well signposted
CONTACT TEL. NUMBERS	R C National Shrine Pilgrim Bureau Friday Market Place Little Walsingham Norfolk ENGLAND NR22 6EG Tel. Bureau 01328 820217 Shrine 01328 820495 Shrine shop 01328 821794
EMAIL ADDRESS	rcnationalshrine@walsingham.org.uk
WEB SITE	www.walsingham.org.uk
TIMES OF SERVICES	PROGRAMME OF RELIGIOUS ACTIVITY (Easter to October) WEEKDAYS 11.00–11.45 – Sacrament of Reconciliation – Chapel of Reconciliation 12.00 – Angelus and PILGRIM MASS – Chapel of Reconciliation 2.30pm – Rosary – Slipper Chapel 3.00pm – Adoration of the Blessed Sacrament – Chapel of Reconciliation 4.00pm – Evening Prayer and Benediction – Chapel of Reconciliation WEEKENDS 11.00–11.45 – Sacrament of Reconciliation – Chapel of Reconciliation 12.00 – Angelus and PILGRIM MASS – Chapel of Reconciliation 2.00pm – Adoration of the Blessed Sacrament 3.00pm – Benediction – Chapel of Reconciliation 5.00pm – (*SUNDAYS ONLY*) Mass – The Shrine

SPECIAL DATES/ EVENTS/ FESTIVALS/ PILGRIMAGES	The calendar for pilgrimages, feast days, etc is very full, with a huge variety of activities; some of the special ones are:
	25 March: Solemnity of the Annunciation of the Lord (Marian Feast)
	31 May: The visitation of the B.V.M.
	1st Tuesday of July: Union of Catholic Mothers Pilgrimage (2007 was the 62nd annual pilgrimage)
	July: Tamil Pilgrimage (7000 usually attend)
	July: Pilgrimage for children, with parents and grandparents, Sunday nearest the Feast of SS Joachim and Anne
	15 August: Solemnity of the Assumption of the B.V.M.
	7 September: The Dowry of Mary Pilgrimage
	24 September: Solemnity of our Lady of Walsingham
	8 December: Solemnity of the Immaculate Conception of the B.V.M.
	The Walsingham Association exists primarily to spread devotion to Our Lady of Walsingham and encourage pilgrimage to her Shrine; to join contact 01328 820217
ANGLICAN CHURCH AND CONTACT TEL. NUMBERS	The Anglican Shrine of Our Lady of Walsingham Tel. 01328 820255
GOOD PUBS	Fakenham, 4 miles away, and Walsingham village, have a good selection of hotels, pubs, tea-shops, restaurants and inns

PLACES FOR PILGRIMS TO STAY	ELMHAM HOUSE Tel. 01328 820217 elmhamhouse@walsingham.org.uk
	Anglican Shrine of Our Lady also has accommodation, tel. 01328 820239

24

Warwick Street

WARWICK STREET

Like an enclosed garden in the middle of a jungle, Golden Square lies in the centre of London, surrounded by the glitter of Regent Street, the narrow lanes and the bustling Chinese restaurants of Soho. At number 24 the presbytery of the church of Our Lady of the Assumption and St Gregory stands among the fine Georgian buildings that edge the square.

The church fronts on to Warwick Street which runs parallel with the western side of the Square, and the story is one of Catholic survival in London during the penal times. By the end of the eighteenth century public veneration was once more possible and the shrine of Our Lady of the Assumption became a landmark in this part of London, as people came in increasing numbers to pray before her statue. The shrine is frequently and affectionately known as Our Lady of Warwick Street.

In the centre of Golden Square, there is a garden planted out beneath the gaze of King George II, whose statue stands with pigeons for company. This strange figure – for no-one knows for certain how he found his way here – gives some hint of the history of the area, and in particular of the story of the sole remaining embassy chapel, built in England at the beginning of the eighteenth century.

In December 1784, George II's great-grandson, the future George IV, went through a form of marriage with the Catholic Mrs Fitzherbert, which a Catholic would recognize, but which was not valid in English law. Mrs Fitzherbert lived in the area and prayed in the small Bavarian embassy chapel. Her husband, the Prince of Wales, was seldom on good terms with his father, the unfortunate George III, who refused to allow his Prime Minister William Pitt 'the Younger' to bring in a measure of Catholic Emancipation in 1801, because he believed this to be in breach of his coronation oath.

The Square has not always appeared to be so hemmed-in by its neighbours, nor has the air of peaceful gentility seemed so comfortably established. Long before Regent Street was built, the area of Golden Square was used as a pasture for geldings, and during the reign of Charles II it was known as Gelding Close.

During the years of the great plague in the middle of the seventeenth century, the area to the north near Marshall Street was used as a burial ground. A notorious workhouse was built nearby when the plague subsided, and to the south Brewer Street owes its name to all the breweries that once thrived in the area.

Warwick Street lay on the direct route from the City to Tyburn, and the rising flood-waters each year caused chaos for many who travelled this way, and for those whose poverty left them little choice of where to live.

In 1673, ambitious plans for a new square were approved by Sir Christopher Wren, and the atmosphere of disease and poverty was dispelled. A new elegance emerged as the square was completed in the early 1700s and gradually the fashionable and diplomatic *monde* moved in.

GOLDEN SQUARE

In 1724, the Portuguese embassy arrived at numbers 23 and 24 Golden Square, where the envoy built a Catholic chapel, between the house and the stables, which also had access on to Warwick Street. In 1747 the Portuguese departed for Mayfair and the Bavarians took their place. The Bavarian envoy and his successors maintained the chapel with devoted care, and it became known as the 'Bavarian Chapel'.

It would be difficult to overestimate the importance of the embassy chapels during the seventeenth and eighteenth centuries, when the everyday practice of their faith was becoming well-nigh impossible for Catholics living in London.

Penal Times

While the majority of the population accepted the new dispensation under the supremacy of King Henry VIII, those who were determined to remain Catholic faced constant danger and found themselves restricted by increasingly punitive legislation.

The penal laws began under Queen Elizabeth I. The state of recusancy was defined as failure to attend the parish church, and it was penalized with increasingly heavy fines. The means of earning a livelihood was prescribed by an extraordinarily detailed list of employments forbidden to Catholics, including medicine, pleading in court and service in the armed forces. To be a Catholic landowner could mean financial ruin and the forfeiture of estates to a conforming relation. Men were excluded from both Houses of Parliament, and forbidden to bear arms.

After the Restoration of the Monarchy in 1660, the Test Act of 1672 required all holders of office under the Crown, including Members of Parliament, to receive the Eucharist according to the usage of the Church of England. The Act also required holders of office to make formal declaration against the doctrine of Transubstantiation.

In 1685 matters seemed to be improving for Catholics with the accession of the Catholic James II; however, three years later James lost the throne to his Protestant daughter Mary and her husband, William of Orange.

In 1689, the Bill of Rights further curtailed the lives of Catholics. By now they were debarred from inheriting or purchasing land and forbidden to keep arms, ammunition or a horse worth more than ten pounds. Priests were to be punished with imprisonment for life for celebrating Mass, and spies who secured the conviction of a priest were offered a reward of £100. Catholics were unable to practise law and prohibited from sending their children abroad for education. They were also prohibited from living within ten miles of London. While it is difficult to be accurate about figures, it is believed that sixty thousand Catholics remained in England. It is a testament to their stamina that twenty thousand of these remained in London.

Eventually the apostasy and, in some cases, the financial ruin of many of the wealthy Catholic families led to the closure of their private chapels. The diplomatic representatives in England of the Catholic powers from across the water became a life-line to their co-religionists in London. By creating embassy chapels and providing chaplains for their envoys, the survival of the Catholic faith was ensured almost within sight of the Houses of Parliament, whose Members were busy devising laws to bring about its demise. Diplomatic representation included the provision of a Catholic chaplain who would make himself available, not only to the staff of the Embassy, but to the local population.

However, this close alliance with the embassies of many of England's enemies during the eighteenth century did little to allay the deep suspicion with which Catholics were already viewed. In 1778 the first 'Catholic Relief Act' was introduced, and immediately opposed by Lord George Gordon, who promptly summoned the Protestant Association to action.

In what became known as the Gordon Riots, on 2 June 1779 gangs gathered to attack Members of Parliament as they arrived at the House: the mob led by the fanatical Gordon then went on the rampage to destroy any Catholic property they could find. Supporters carried flags with the legend 'No Popery'. London was in turmoil for ten days. The chapel of the Bavarian embassy was attacked and most of the contents thrown into the street and burned: the Portuguese coat of arms was torn from the ceiling. Although the damage was extensive, the chapel was not destroyed, and in the following year a committee was formed to begin the repairs.

To increase the size of the chapel, the stables were pulled down, and the building then stretched from the Embassy at 23 and 24 Golden Square to a new frontage on Warwick Street which already gave entrance to the chapel. In 1790 it was reopened and dedicated to St Gregory the Great. In later years the enlarged chapel was to be criticized for the austerity of its design, but at the end of the eighteenth century the memory of penal times was still a painful reality, and the intention was to create an exterior that was unassuming and unlikely to attract attention.

The French Revolution of 1789 brought fugitive Catholics to England, both clergy and laity, and many of them remained in London. The Bavarian chapel became fashionable and, in a portent of things to come, the traffic was frequently brought to a standstill by the increase in the number of carriages. In 1793 a Requiem Mass was sung in the chapel for King Louis XVI of France and his Queen, Marie Antoinette.

At the beginning of the nineteenth century the future Duke of Wellington attended the chapel in order to give away the American bride of his aide-de-camp. John Henry Newman came to Warwick Street as a boy, and in 1853 the Stuart Society arranged a Requiem Mass for the Queen of Portugal; the subsequent drawing of the chapel in the *Illustrated London News* gives a fascinating picture of the interior at that time. In 1861, the explorer Richard Burton married his Catholic bride Isabel Arundell at Warwick Street.

In 1884 the name of the church was expanded to include a dedication to Our Lady of the Assumption. Although the Blessed Virgin had been held in special devotion here for many years, the change of title was apparently prompted by the acquisition of a fine panel depicting the Assumption, by the sculptor John Edward Carew, which is now installed over the doorway to the left of the altar.

Walking along Warwick Street today, with the roar of traffic in Regent Street nearby, and the hurrying groups of office workers, Starbucks' coffee in hand, one comes with surprise upon the plain façade of the church. And yet this unassuming exterior conceals a breathtaking interior with exquisite mosaics above the altar, and a fine gallery to accommodate large congregations.

The shrine of Our Lady of the Assumption stands on the epistle side of the altar. The statue of the Blessed Virgin is a French copy of the figure in the church in the Rue du Bac in Paris where the nineteenth-century Sister of Charity, St Catherine Labouré, received visions of Our Lady in a form that was later reproduced on the 'Miraculous Medal'. In 1954 on 8 December, the Feast of the Immaculate Conception, the London statue was crowned by the Archbishop of Westminster, Cardinal Bernard Griffin.

As the shrine became increasingly popular, the continental habit of presenting silver hearts in thanksgiving for prayers answered was adopted here, and at one time these filled no less than thirty-seven cases. Today their number has been radically reduced to two panels, which stand on either side of the statue.

The nature of the congregation has altered dramatically over the years. At the end of the nineteenth century, the area was heavily populated – a busy and flourishing community with its own schools originally supported by the Bavarian envoy and subsequently adopted by the Westminster diocese.

With the growth of commerce in the area, the character has inevitably altered, and with it the needs of the Catholic community. During the Second World War many parishioners left London, and their places were taken by servicemen of the United States, Canada and the Free French.

Since the war the resident Catholic population has diminished, but the congregation has increased with the large number of Italian and Irish employees in the local catering industry. Thus, the original chapel of the Portuguese Envoy remains true to its vocation, to provide spiritual sustenance for those who come to England from Europe, as well as for those who live nearby.

Shrine – Warwick Street

LOCATION/ DIRECTIONS	London Underground Bakerloo/Piccadilly line Piccadilly Circus Station Exit West Side to Regent Street Turn right into Glasshouse Street Left into Warwick Street Church of Our Lady can be found on the right- hand side (10 minute walk from Piccadilly)
CONTACT TEL. NUMBERS	Our Lady of the Assumption and St Gregory The Presbytery 24 Golden Square (rear of church in Warwick Street) London W1F 9JR Tel. 020 7437 1525
EMAIL ADDRESS	warwickstreet@rcdow.org.uk
TIMES OF SERVICES	MASS Sunday: Sat 6.00pm (first mass of Sunday) 10.30am, 5.00pm Monday to Friday: 12.45pm Holy Days: 8.00am, 12.15pm, 12.45pm and 5.45pm Sacrament of Reconciliation Monday to Friday 12.15pm–12.35pm and after Mass Saturday 5.15pm–5.45pm
SPECIAL DATES/ EVENTS/ FESTIVALS/ PILGRIMAGES	Celebrate the feast of our Lady of Assumption, 15 August

ANGLICAN CHURCH AND CONTACT TEL. NUMBERS	St James 197 Piccadilly London W1J 9LL Tel. 020 7734 4511 www.stjames.piccadilly.org
LOCAL ATTRACTIONS	4 West End Roman Catholic Churches, including Warwick Street; Corpus Christi at Covent Garden; St Patrick's near Tottenham Court Road; and Notre Dame de France, off Leicester Square Piccadilly Circus, Carnaby Street, Trafalgar Square, West End theatres, Regent Street/Oxford Street/New Bond Street shopping!
GOOD PUBS	Good choice of cafés, restaurants and accommodation within this area

THE PRIESTS HOUSE, WEST GRINSTEAD

25

West Grinstead

WEST GRINSTEAD

My visit to the shrine of Our Lady of Consolation at West Grinstead was on a day of watery January sunshine: mist was rising from the surrounding fields, and the imposing church of Our Lady of Consolation and St Francis appeared to be standing in the middle of nowhere; its only neighbours are the fine thirteenth-century Anglican parish church of St George, and a few cottages.

It is a place that appears to be quintessentially English, and yet this is misleading. In the nineteenth century, this church was founded by a Frenchman, and one of his compatriots, Hilaire

Belloc, made this his spiritual home for nearly forty-five years in the twentieth century.

This out-of-the-way shrine was the first to be established in England in honour of the Blessed Virgin after the Reformation. While other shrines had languished, waiting for their rescue after centuries of neglect, the shrine of Our Lady at West Grinstead was created at the end of the nineteenth century in thanksgiving for the continous thread of faith in this corner of Sussex. Even today the atmosphere is decidedly recusant.

This shrine lies in the heart of West Sussex, close to the site of West Grinstead Park, the home of the Caryll family whose courage and determination preserved this hidden place during the Reformation and for many years afterwards. On this January day, there was a sense of quiet watchfulness that cannot be dispelled despite the years that separate us from those times of danger so long ago – perhaps it is the winter's mist that summons ghosts to the imagination. The noise of traffic on the road from Horsham to Worthing seemed to come from another world.

Little evidence remains of the great estate and moated manor house of West Grinstead which was home to the Carylls in the reign of Queen Elizabeth I. Originally from Ireland, their estates extended across Sussex and into Hampshire. The family came to the attention of the authorities in 1580 when a surprise search was made for two suspected priests, both of whom remained undiscovered, undoubtedly because of a local unwillingness to betray the Carylls. After the Gunpowder Plot of 1605 life became increasingly dangerous for Catholic priests, and the Carylls were obliged to close the chapel adjoining their house.

The need for safe hiding places prompted ingenious solutions. Under cover of darkness, stones were carried across the fields to a small cottage that stood hidden amongst woodland. Four new rooms were created, a 'secret' chapel with a concealed entrance was constructed in the hay loft, and hiding places were concealed in the wide chimney flues. Edward Caryll wished this building to be a mission for the people of the neighbourhood, and for over two hundred years the little attic chapel became a Mass centre for the surrounding area.

The cottage was originally a stockman's dwelling, and the biblical associations were fully exploited as priests travelled the countryside disguised as shepherds.

West Grinstead Park lay a mere eighteen miles from the south coast and was on the main road to London, which made it an important safe haven for priests crossing from the Continent. As they reached the River Adur the priests would look to the reed-cutters for the one who would ensure them safe passage. Their man would be the one who cut his reed by slicing down the stem and then across the root, thus forming a sign of the cross.

Some years later, a crippled reed-cutter came to the priests' house and, finding it in need of tidying, laid down his sticks and began the task with a prayer to the Virgin. Then and there he was miraculously cured, and his crutches are left to this day in the priests' house.

Among the many priests who served at the mission at West Grinstead was the Franciscan Francis Bell, who was martyred at Tyburn in 1643. The indictment included 'saying Mass at West Grinstead'. Among the treasured relics in the church is the silver chalice that belonged to the martyr, together with his last letter.

The fortunes of the Carylls fluctuated with their determination to maintain the old faith. Several members of the family became priests or nuns, but there were times when the constant awareness of danger and the imposition of punitive fines became almost too much to bear for those with families to consider. In 1671 John Caryll's anxiety for the safety of his wife and nine children overcame him, and he signed the Oath of Allegiance. He soon regretted this, and subsequently paid £600 towards the upkeep of three priests at West Grinstead.

In 1678 a Popish plot was said to have been uncovered by the conspirator Titus Oates, against 'His Sacred Majesty King Charles II, the government and the entire Protestant Religion.' This inflamed public opinion; however, no evidence has ever been found to justify his accusation that Catholics were plotting to assassinate the King, and Oates was eventually discredited. But the damage had been done. Heightened anxiety resulted in increased taxation upon Catholics and the withdrawal of many of their civil rights. Such harassment eventually brought down a number of them.

In 1688 John Caryll (the seventh of that name) followed the Catholic King James II into exile in France. He was never able to return. In 1754 his great-nephew, another John, was forced to sell West Grinstead Park for £6,000, but not before he had ensured the future of the priests' house with an endowment of £1,300 to the Franciscans to pay for the maintenance of a chaplain.

The Franciscans remained at West Grinstead until 1815 and were followed by French émigré priests. The inability of these priests to make themselves understood in English may have accelerated the decline in local Catholic practice, and the mission seemed to be on the verge of closure. In 1863 this state of affairs was substantially improved by the arrival of Monsignor Jean-Marie Denis. The scene that greeted him was discouraging, to say the least, and it was some years before the Monsignor could make much headway. The chapel was in poor condition: there had been little or no money since the breakup of the Caryll estate, and the few parishioners were widely scattered. The local bishop reassured Monsignor Denis with the words, 'The mission has nothing to fear – it has seen far harder times. It has protection in heaven and you will see at West Grinstead things that will surprise you'.

Monsignor Denis maintained his links with France and was there in 1870 at the time of the Franco-Prussian war. He travelled to Versailles, and through his pleading on their behalf several Bretons were saved from execution. The gratitude of the people of Brittany was to fill the coffers of West Grinstead, when Monsignor Denis visited them on a future occasion seeking funds for his building projects there. Returning to England with the necessary money, he embarked upon an ambitious building plan for a school and a new church: the Victorian Gothic edifice was completed in 1876, and is dedicated to Our Lady of Consolation and St Francis. Angels bearing the armorial shields of the families associated with the early chapel grace the capitals beneath the fine vaulted ceiling.

Monsignor Denis' next project was a shrine in honour of Our Lady, and he set off for Europe once more, this time for Italy, and the shrine of the *Consolata* in Turin. The title of Our Lady of Consolation was one that was familiar and venerated in England before the Reformation: the icon of the *Consolata* had been brought from the Holy Land in the fourth century by St Eusebius, for presentation to the Bishop of Turin. It had survived countless perils on the long journey, which was perhaps the source of its appeal to Monsignor Denis. He arranged for a copy of the *Consolata* icon to be painted for the West Grinstead shrine and it was brought back to England and installed beneath a canopy to the left of the altar.

Monsignor Denis intended that this should be the shrine, but the situation was complicated by an Indult of the Vatican Chapter for the solemn coronation of 'Our Lady of Consolation of West Grinstead'. Since it was not possible to crown a picture, a figure of Our Lady was carved, similar to the one on the copied icon of the *Consolata*. This statue stands in a niche above the main altar, surrounded by a stone reredos depicting scenes from the life of the Blessed Virgin. In 1893 it became the first image of Our Lady to be publicly crowned in England since the Reformation, and at the same time, Pope Leo XIII granted autonomy to the shrine.

By the time of Monsignor Denis's death in 1900, there had been a pilgrimage from Horsham to the shrine: the first of many such pilgrimages which continue to the present day. On the site of the old school a covered area has recently been created for pilgrims who wish to picnic. Monsignor Denis was able to leave a well-established church and school, and also a convent for the Dominican nuns who ran the school. In acknowledgement of their contribution to the parish, the window in the east aisle shows the Blessed Virgin handing a rosary to St Dominic, and in the graveyard several crosses commemorate the nuns.

The graveyard is also the burial place of Hilaire Belloc, who lived in the area for nearly forty-five years. He rests close to his beloved South Downs, and the burial place is overloooked by the tower built in his memory in 1964. A few miles away, in the village of Shipley, there is a handsome windmill that has been carefully restored in his memory.

The novelist Antonia White also lies here and the portrait painter, Sir James Gunn, has a fine stone carving of a Madonna and Child on his grave.

At the beginning of the twenty-first century, new life is being breathed into the shrine with the appointment of a former Anglican priest, Father David Goddard, as chaplain, and with meagre resources an inspiring programme of restoration is underway.

The priests' house is a strange mixture of Tudor walls with blackened timbers and Victorian brick. Images of the Mysteries of the Rosary have recently been placed in the garden by the Rosary Way Trust, and in the distance a figure of Mary stands beneath spreading trees. On the day of my visit, the 'secret chapel' in the priest's house was undergoing minor restoration, and ears of corn had been found beneath the floorboards, a reminder that this had once been a hayloft. The chapel is used daily in the winter, and is constantly visited by pilgrims and by children from nearby schools. As I stood in the tiny room I was overwhelmed by an awareness of the dangers facing those who prayed here so many centuries ago, and of the solace they found in this place.

The shine of Our Lady of Consolation of West Grinstead vividly preserves the memory of the Catholic faith in times of persecution. Many of today's pilgrims may be unaware of its history, because it is also a shrine for today which offers an inspiring programme of prayer and meditation in glorious surroundings.

Shrine – Our Lady of Consolation, West Grinstead

LOCATION/ DIRECTIONS	From M25, exit J9 A24 towards Horsham/Worthing Turn left to Partridge Green, B2135 1 mile on l/h side, Our Lady of Consolation Shrine
CONTACT TEL. NUMBERS	The Priest House, Park Lane West Grinstead Horsham RH13 8LT West Sussex Tel. 01403 710273
EMAIL ADDRESS	revdavidgoddard@ukonline.co.uk
TIMES OF SERVICES	MASS Monday and Saturday 9.00am Wednesday 12.00 noon Sunday Masses 6.00pm Saturday Vigil Mass 10.30am Parish Mass Sacrament of Penance 5.30pm on Saturday or by appointment The Tridentine Mass is usually celebrated at 3.00pm one Sunday a month. Phone for details or contact the Latin Mass Society.
SPECIAL DATES/ EVENTS/ FESTIVALS/ PILGRIMAGES	Easter to October is the main pilgrim season; please contact the priest for more details
ROSARY GROUP	Rosary Walk in Shrine Garden
ANGLICAN CHURCH AND CONTACT TEL. NUMBERS	The Parish Church of St George (dates back to 11th century) West Grinstead Tel. 01403 710339

LOCAL ATTRACTIONS	Belloc lies buried in the shrine church yard Secret chapel at the Presbytery, visits by arrangement
	Shipley Windmill (restricted opening times)
GOOD PUBS	The Windmill, Littleworth (5 min. drive)
PLACES FOR PILGRIMS TO STAY	St Cuthmans (retreat run by Diocese of Arundel & Brighton) Tel. 01403 741220 www.stcuthmans.com

26

Westminster

Our Lady of Pew

'Would you like to visit the private chapel for prayer?' a gentle voice asked me. I was sitting in Westminster Abbey on steps leading to the chapel of Edward the Confessor, once the greatest shrine in England, and now sadly closed to the general public unless accompanied by a guide. It is however open one day a year for the celebration of the Ransom Mass on the nearest day to his feast.

Unable to enter the chapel of the Confessor, I also refuse the kind invitation to visit the private chapel and remain seated on the steps, watching the crowds drift to and fro apparently dazed by the complexity of the story that wafts across from the guide leading them past monuments and tombs, chapels and chantries and all the tantalizing muddle of our island history. A woman passes the statue of the Blessed Virgin, pauses and gently touches it before she too wanders away. There is even the jangle of a mobile phone adding plaintively to the cacophony, until the prayer which is said every hour, on the hour, brings silence and a momentary pause.

In front of me, between the chapel of St John and the chantry chapel built by the sixteenth-century abbot of Westminster, John Islip, there stands the twentieth-century alabaster figure of the Lady of Pew. The statue glows in the candle-light in what appears to be a small passageway, but is in fact a tiny chantry chapel. The vaulted ceiling is decorated with stars surrounding a carved boss of the Assumption of Our Lady. Behind the statue recess, above the new alabaster figure, the faded markings of a white hart are faintly visible, the badge of King Richard II.

Looking down on this scene is a small carved image of the Green Man, who has been smiling through many centuries on those who have visited the shrine of Our Lady. Despite all that goes on around it, the chantry chapel radiates an air of sanctity. The outer doorway with its heavily-carved wooden panels still bears the iron brackets for tapers or alms boxes and on either side of the entrance are angels holding the coats of arms of Richard II and St Edward the Confessor.

Across the north ambulatory there lies the tomb of the man in whose memory this chapel was endowed. Aymer de Valence, Earl of Pembroke, died in 1324 after only three years of marriage to his Countess, Mary de St Pole. For the remaining fifty-three years of her life Mary mourned his loss, endowing numerous religious foundations in his memory. Shortly before her death in 1377 she made a bequest creating this chantry, leaving instructions in her will that a monk should sing daily here – 'near the place of burial of my very dear lord, Sir Aymer de Valance ... and to keep the anniversaries both of him and of myself'. Included in her gift was a statue of the Virgin Mary. The brackets that held the alabaster statue can still be seen, although the figure vanished in the sixteenth century.

At the time of Lady Pembroke's endowment of the chantry chapel in Westminster Abbey there was a shrine named 'Our Lady of le Pewe' within the precincts of the Palace of Westminster. The origin of the name may go back to the thirteenth century when King Henry III ordered that an image of the Blessed Virgin be painted on the outside of the King's Pew at St Stephen's chapel. Over the years there have been other suggestions as to the origin of this title. The word 'puits' for wells seemed a possibility as there were no less than four wells beside St Stephen's chapel; the nineteenth-century antiquary Edmund Waterton suggested that the word may have been taken from 'Our Lady of Pity' shortened by a careless scribe to 'pty' and thence to 'pui'; according to another source, the word derives from the French shrine of Our Lady of Puy. Whatever the origin of the name might have been, this building was destroyed by fire in 1452 when a careless schoolboy failed to extinguish all the candles before the statue. The restored chapel of St Stephen now lies within the Houses of Parliament.

The title of 'Our Lady of Pewe' was therefore familiar and honoured in Westminster when the Countess of Pembroke founded her chantry within the Abbey, and it would have appeared to be a logical choice.

Originally this little chapel was a self-contained area entered through the chapel of St John. In 1503, work began on Henry VII's magnificent chapel, which he intended to be the finest Lady chapel in England. Devotion to Our Lady diminished in the little chapel of Pew, and for three hundred years it was known as the chapel of St Erasmus. The survival of the decoration of the chapel was believed to be due in part to the protection of St Erasmus, whose statue stood above the doorway.

In 1523 the entrance was blocked by the tomb of Bishop Ruthall of Durham, the Lord Privy Seal, who died of shame having mistakenly sent Henry VIII a list of his own possessions, rather than the state papers the King expected. The chapel was then realigned and became a recess in the entrance to St John's chapel and today, seen from the foot of the bishop's tomb, the newly-installed figure of Our Lady of Pew glows with an extraordinary light.

Our Lady's Dowry

The English kings up to the time of the Reformation undoubtedly honoured Our Lady of Pew and prayed for her protection. Beside the majestic tomb of the Confessor decorated with figures of the saints, lie the bodies of King Richard II and his first wife, Anne of Bohemia. One can imagine these magnificent monarchs gathering in the shadows of the abbey after the last of the crowds have wandered away, to discuss times gone by; recalling their triumphs and disasters. Perhaps they are unperturbed by the strange company in which they now find themselves, the triumphant politicians of a later age whose great monuments line the entrance. These men have their gaze fixed on horizons soon to be conquered – but seldom in a spirit of Christian charity.

The monarchs and politicians in Westminster Abbey perhaps have more in common than might at first seem apparent: shared ambition, certainly, but also a great love for their country.

By the great west door of the abbey hangs a portrait of King Richard II who gazes at all who enter this place. Richard was only ten when he inherited the crown from his grandfather, Edward III. In the picture he looks very young and his youthful solemnity is impressive. His eyes are averted from the beholder, his hand holding lightly the golden orb as if he already realises that his tenure of the throne was likely to be short; it is far from peaceful.

During the Peasants' Revolt of 1381 large crowds of protesting citizens descended on London in a scene of riot and upheaval that is only too familiar today. The patience of the impoverished populace had finally been exhausted by the introduction of a swingeing poll tax. The King and his court were besieged in the Tower of London, and the mob beheaded the unfortunate Simon of Sudbury, Archbishop of Canterbury and Chancellor of England, who was held responsible for the despised tax.

Under their leader, Wat Tyler, there seemed little to stop the protesters. Whatever else may have been questioned about Richard's reign, the young King's courage was never in doubt. The thirteen-year-old monarch came out to meet his people at Smithfield to listen to their woes and to attempt to bring calm in the face of a potential bloodbath.

Wat Tyler raised his arm as if to bring down his sword upon Richard, who responded: 'Surely you do not mean to kill your king?' He listened to the crowd, promised his assistance, and bade them depart in peace to their homes. Richard's commitment to his people was later betrayed by the politicians who lost no time in grasping the temporary advantage gained by the king's intervention. Wat Tyler was murdered and many others were hanged, but such reprisals were never held to be the fault of Richard and his brave stand was not forgotten.

Before setting out for Smithfield on the morning of his meeting with the protesters, Richard had risen early and visited the shrine of Saint Edward the Confessor in Westminster Abbey. In the early morning light and before the onslaught of the day he knelt in prayer for his people and asked that his own courage might not fail. He sought the intercession of the Blessed Virgin and it is conjectured that he did so at the shrine of 'le Pewe' – Our Lady of the Pew – in St Stephen's chapel. It was here that he had dedicated his life to the Blessed Virgin on his accession to the throne. This shrine was well known as the place of devotion for the kings of England, whereas the little shrine founded by the Countess of Pembroke within the Abbey, confusingly of the same name, had only existed for three years when the Peasants' Revolt took place. Yet it stood only inches away from the shrine of the Confessor and Richard must have passed by on his way.

After the successful conclusion of the meeting with the protesters Richard did not forget his prayer to the Blessed Virgin and returned to give thanks for her intercession. It was at this time that England became the acknowledged Dowry of Our Lady. The title has never been revoked although it fell into disuse after the Reformation.

In the Wilton Diptych, the imaginary scene of the young King kneeling before the Queen of Heaven is exquisitely depicted in glowing colours by an unknown artist. The Diptych is presently in the keeping of London's National Gallery. From the eighteenth century until 1929 it was housed at Wilton, near Salisbury, the home of the Earls of Pembroke.

King Richard is the focus of attention, which suggests that he may have commissioned the work himself. He is kneeling before the Blessed Virgin, who is surrounded by eleven angels. The Virgin is looking across at him, while her Child leans towards him at such a sharp angle that his Mother holds on to his small foot. The angels, some of whom point towards him, are wearing Richard's emblem, the white hart. It was the custom for supporters of the King to be allowed to wear his badge, so the implication is that the angels were on his side. The number of the angels reflects the age of the young King when he acceded to the throne, in his eleventh year.

The Holy Child is held in his Mother's arms, beneath the banner of England, and on the silver globe above there is a tiny painting of an island surrounded by sea with a small boat sailing past. The young King is presented to the Virgin by St John the Baptist, by the ninth-century King of East Anglia, St Edmund, and by St Edward the Confessor. Within the abbey the chapels of these great saints surround the tombs of King Richard and his Queen, Anne of Bohemia, in the exact sequence of their portrayal in the Wilton Diptych.

The Diptych is believed to echo an earlier altarpiece which survived for several centuries, and is known to have hung at one time in the English College in Rome. In this picture, Richard and Anne were shown kneeling before the Blessed Virgin. Beneath them were the words 'This is your dowry, O Holy Virgin: therefore rule over it, O Mary'. The lost altarpiece and the Wilton Diptych have for centuries encouraged the belief that this little shrine is the heart and centre of Our Lady's Dowry.

The barely-visible image of the white hart above the altar, and the heraldic combination on either side of the door, suggest that this little chapel was used for private devotion by King Richard II, and that the Wilton Diptych was created as an altarpiece for this shrine. Although there were earlier indications that England was the possession of Our Lady as her dowry, this became generally acknowledged during the reign of Richard II. At the King's request, a mandate was issued by Thomas Arundel, Archbishop of Canterbury, in 1399 which included the words: 'we, as the humble servants of her own inheritance and liegeman of her especial dower . . . ought to excel all others in the fervour of our praises and devotions to her'.

The Restored Shrine

For four hundred years the niche in Westminster Abbey which had held the statue of Our Lady remained empty. In the mid-twentieth century Mr Albert Joseph Freeman appeared on the scene. Mr Freeman had fought in the First World War, during which he had been severely gassed. As he lay dying in a field hospital, Albert promised Our Lady that if he recovered, he would spend the rest of his life in her service. He survived, and on a visit to Westminster Abbey the empty niche in the Pew chapel affected him deeply, and he vowed to place a statue in this once-famous shrine.

Despite the complexity of the project Albert Freeman remained determined. He wanted the statue to be created by hands that could not only wield a chisel but were inspired by prayer. The obvious choice of sculptor was therefore Sister Concordia at Minster Abbey.

The difficulties were considerable. Sister Concordia was approached, and was eventually able to visit Westminster Abbey. Little was known of the appearance of the original statue of Our Lady of Pew, but in nearby Westminster Cathedral a fifteenth-century alabaster figure of the Blessed Virgin, known as Our Lady of Power, had recently been installed. This statue was thought to be of the Nottingham school, which was the undoubted source of the original statue of Our Lady of Pew. Sister Concordia decided that the proposed statue in Westminster Abbey should be based upon the figure of Our Lady of Power. The principal difference between the two was the substitution of a rose for a sceptre. Our Lady of Pew should carry a rose to signify love rather than a sceptre to signify strength.

Numerous enquiries were made, but more than two years passed before a sufficiently large and faultless piece of alabster could be found. In November 1969 a suitable block was discovered beneath an old cloth in a studio in Nottingham, and it was arranged that it should be delivered to Sister Concordia at Minster Abbey. Through the rain that fell on the day of its arrival, Sister Concordia could see the gradations in the colouring of the alabaster. The weight of the piece was such that she had to make an immediate decision as to the way in which the stone should be unloaded into her studio, for there could be no question of moving it again.

The upper part of the block was clear and flowed into rich colour, which would be transformed into the folds of drapery below the knees of the carved figure. In the words of the sculptor: 'The Virgin's eyes are closed – she is pondering these things in her heart. The Word is sitting on her knees and the Child is looking at his Father. The Virgin holds a rose, symbol of love.' On the back of the statue are carved the words, 'That they all may be one in Us'.

On 10 March 1971 the statue was installed in Westminster

Abbey. The solemn procession included the Dean of Westminster and four canons, Sister Concordia and her Benedictine abbess, Mother Walburga, and the Apostolic Delegate. At the conclusion of evensong, the choir sang the Ave Maria to a seventeenth-century setting and the procession moved into the Pew chapel, where the statue was unveiled and blessed. The only person who was missing from this gathering was the moving spirit behind it. Albert Freeman had died a few days previously.

The statue is now the focus of the flourishing Society of Our Lady of Pew founded some twenty years ago by the Warden of the Abbey, Mrs Maureen Jupp.

As dusk fell on the day of my visit, the crowds began to leave the abbey. Several people turned to look back towards the statue, radiant in the evening light. I was reluctant to leave, aware of all the great men and women, kings and commoners, poets and soldiers, and all the saints who fill this place. But most of all I was aware that Our Lady had returned to her ancient seat in the abbey of Westminster, and from there she looks upon England, her Dowry.

Shrine – Westminster – Our Lady of Pew

LOCATION/ DIRECTIONS	London Underground, Circle/District Line, Westminster Station, leave at exit 4. Westminster Abbey directly opposite
CONTACT TEL. NUMBERS	Our Lady of Pew C/o Westminster Abbey 20 Deans Yard Westminster London SW1P 3PA Tel. 020 7222 5152
EMAIL ADDRESS	Info@westminster-abbey.org
WEB SITE	www.westminster-abbey.org
TIMES OF SERVICES	Services at Our Lady of Pew: The last Friday of each month at 6.00pm in the Lady Chapel (for approx. 45 minutes) followed by a social gathering afterwards; to include May (Eucharist in honour of Our Lady) July (Eucharist and procession around the abbey) November (requiem followed by AGM of the Society)

Westminster Abbey

Sundays
8.00am Holy Communion, 10.00am Matins, 11.15am Sung Eucharist, 3.00pm Evensong, 5.45pm Organ Recital, 6.30pm Evening Service

Weekdays
7.30am Matins, 8.00am and 12.30pm Holy Communion, 5.00pm Evensong

Saturdays
8.00am Holy Communion, 9.00am Matins, 3.00pm Evensong

Admission charges apply when visiting Westminster Abbey, but if you would like to visit the shrine to say prayers only, a marshal will take you there at no charge.

SPECIAL DATES/ EVENTS/ FESTIVALS/ PILGRIMAGES	Pilgrimages can be arranged for groups; contact 20 Dean's Yard.
ROMAN CATHOLIC AND CONTACT TEL. NUMBERS	Westminster Cathedral 42 Francis Street London SW1P 1QW Tel. 020 7798 9055 Service times 020 7798 9097 The nearest tube and train station is Victoria
LOCAL ATTRACTIONS	London Eye Houses of Parliament Big Ben The Wilton Diptych can be seen in the Sainsbury Wing of the National Gallery in Trafalgar Square.
GOOD PUBS	Very good choice of bars, restaurants and accommodation in area

27

Willesden

Over the centuries, the pilgrim route to this once-famous shrine in North London has changed beyond recognition. Most of the roads out of London now look the same once the city is left behind, for the old towns and villages have been submerged in a never-ending sprawl of development. This appeared to have been the fate of Willesden.

While the early pilgrims travelled along lanes surrounded by rolling countryside with distant views of Windsor Castle, my own pilgrimage to Willesden began in the labyrinthine tunnels of the London Underground. Apart from an occasional busker, there was little sound other than the tramp of feet as people converged and yet never met; far from the companionable banter of earlier travellers, this was a frenetic and solitary affair.

The long journey took me beneath London, and eventually the train emerged into daylight. The track ran beside grassy banks, and trees shading the last wild flowers of summer. At Willesden Junction I took the road to the shrine through streets of boarded-up shops, cars throbbing with reggae music, and Muslims passing quietly by. A rise in the road led me into the centre of a bustling multicultural street, the shops filled with exotic foods from all over the world. All at once, Willesden emerged as a vibrant home for peoples of differing race and colour, teeming with young families, and on the day of my visit there was an air of carnival which on reflection made the Willesden of today not unlike the great centre of pilgrimage of earlier days.

Along the busy road there walked two girls of Caribbean descent, their hair finely plaited and their dresses glistening in the afternoon sun. Their laughter and chatter filled the air despite the roar of traffic. Their steps took them along the same street I was taking, until they turned into a gate and momentarily pausing, they both genuflected in front of the crucifix beside the church, before continuing their conversation. The lettering over the small gate read 'Our Lady of Willesden'.

Before the Norman conquest this area of forest and marshland belonged to St Paul's Cathedral. Pigs were fattened here for the tables of city clergy. A visitor who was despatched from St Paul's to inspect the property during the thirteenth century noted that there was a little church dedicated to 'Blessed Mary of Willesden', in which there were two large statues of the Blessed Virgin.

After centuries of religious turmoil, there are once again two statues of Our Lady of Willesden and each one is black. Although this may seem appropriate in a place so rich in cultural diversity, it appears that this is not a recent phenomenon, for the shrine was known in medieval times as the 'Black Virgin of Willesden'.

The history of these beautiful statues is a story of its own. 'Black Madonnas' are numerous in Spain, and in the south of France one of the most famous is to be found on the steep cliffside of the Causse de Quercy at Rocamadour. According to Sarah Boss of the Centre for Marian Studies, legend tells of a hermit who had come from the Holy Land and built an oratory against the cliff, which he dedicated to Our Lady. He had brought with him a statue of the Virgin and Child which was believed to have been carved by St Luke. The dark image venerated at Rocamadour today is believed to be that same statue.

Scholars sometimes trace the origins of the statues to the lyrical words of the Song of Songs 'I am black and beautiful, O daughters of Jerusalem' (Song of Songs 1.5). In *Our Lady of Willesden* the Reverend Nicholas Schofield makes the point that some authorities consider the blackness of the statues to be a sign of the sorrow of Mary. According to an Eastern tradition, her darkness is caused by her proximity to the heat of the sun which represents Christ. The origins are veiled in mystery, but the Black Madonnas are believed by their devotees to be a source of miraculous power.

In its early days, the church in Willesden stood peacefully among the trees, surrounded by common land stretching as far as the eye could see. To the west were the marshes of Brent, and the road from Paddington to Harrow ran nearby.

Although the thirteenth century saw the addition of north and south aisles with imposing columns and even a bell tower, by the late fourteenth century enthusiasm had waned to such an extent that the church was described as being in a disgraceful state. The unfortunate vicar was even given permission by the Pope to live elsewhere, so poor and uncomfortable was his living at Willesden.

We shall never know why the first pilgrims were prompted to come to the shrine of Our Lady of Willesden. Perhaps there was a miracle – or the answer to a prayer which was believed to have come about through her intercession.

The name Willesden comes from the Anglo-Saxon 'Wiell-dun' which is believed to mean 'hill of the spring'. There was a well here, as is so often the case at shrines of the Virgin. There were certainly rumours of miracles taking place at the well, and a vision was seen of Our Lady in one of the oak trees in the churchyard. By the end of the fifteenth century, crowds were filling the country lanes on their way to honour the 'Black Virgin of Willesden'.

The fame of the shrine spread rapidly, and the rich and famous left the dirt and grime of London to travel into the country to visit the shrine. In their wake came great numbers of pilgrims, and so too came tradesmen to cater for their needs; the makers of badges, beads and candles – the badge was the sign of the bona fide pilgrim.

Elizabeth of York, the wife of King Henry VII, honoured each feast of Our Lady by making gifts to her favourite shrines. In 1502 she anxiously awaited the birth of her seventh child following a lengthy illness. In that year Elizabeth sent her emissary bearing gifts to some fifteen shrines, including that of Willesden. The story ends sadly with the death of both Elizabeth and her child.

St Thomas More was one of the more famous devotees of Our Lady of Willesden, and came here frequently on pilgrimage. He had an added incentive, for his step-daughter Alice married Sir Giles Alington at Willesden in 1524. Two of More's own daughters were married in the Alington private chapel at Willesden. More's last visit to Willesden took place in 1534 – two weeks before his arrest and imprisonment in the Tower of London.

Very little is known of the appearance of the original statues of Our Lady at Willesden. By the beginning of the sixteenth century reference is made to a single statue. In 1509 Elizabeth Sampson lived with her husband in the city of London, and she mischievously described Our Lady of Willesden as 'a burnt-tailed elf and a burnt tailed stock'; for which she received a sharp rebuke. However, the observation leaves us in no doubt as to the darkness of the wood.

At the time of the Reformation, the statue stood beneath a canopy of silk between the altar and the nave, and was protected by an iron grille. Some scholars doubt the authenticity of the detailed picture of the shrine that is claimed to have been provided by Richard Mores. It is said that Mores was despatched by Henry VIII's chief minister,

Thomas Cromwell, to view the contents of the shrine, and the description is very interesting: 'They have there an image of Our Lady in robes of sarcenet [fine soft silk] with stones; with a veil withal of lace embroidered with pearls and other precious jewels, and gold and silver . . . We did strip the image which we found to be of wood, in colour like ebony, of ancient workmanship, only save the upper parts thoroughly plated in silver.'

As an afterthought, Mores mentions that the place was crowded with pilgrims. He adds, in a revealing aside, 'Even at our coming there were five folk praying before it, two old men and a woman with a child, and one that had brought an offering of flowers'. We are left with one of the few eye-witness accounts of the shrine and of the affection in which it was held by its devotees. The 'folk praying' were presumably unaware of the intentions of this man whom they perhaps took to be a pilgrim like themselves.

A contemporary chronicler reported that the statue of Our Lady of Willesden joined her sister statues in Chelsea, to be consumed in a huge bonfire at the behest of Thomas Cromwell. However, the recent discovery of the statue of Our Lady of Ipswich in Italy at Nettuno leads one to hope that perhaps the Willesden statue also escaped the flames, and is honoured today in some distant place.

For the 'crime' of being 'an idolatrous parish' the King imposed an annual fine of £13 on the incumbent of the church of St Mary. The unfortunate man was fined a further twenty-six shillings for having housed 'an idolatrous image'.

The wills of those who died during the middle years of the sixteenth century make it clear that the shrine was not forgotten, and a number of people still wished to be buried under the protection of Our Lady of Willesden. There was talk of an appearance to a Dr Crewkerne, in which the Blessed Virgin expressed the wish that she might continue to be honoured in Ipswich and at Willesden. Under cross examination about the 'appearance' by Thomas Cranmer, the formidable Archbishop of Canterbury, Crewkehorne courage failed him and he recanted.

Post-Reformation

The church of St Mary became the Anglican parish church and the incumbent continued to pay the fine for 'having housed an idolatrous image'. Gradually the shrine faded from the memory of most people, and Willesden settled back into its country existence, a peaceful backwater, largely untouched by the dramatic events in the city of London which still seemed distant.

But for the remaining Catholics, life was far from peaceful. The lanes that had witnessed the comings and goings of amiable crowds of pilgrims now became the route for priests travelling in disguise to care for their flocks. Sometimes priestly captives passed by under armed guard on their way to torture and death at Tyburn. But devotion to Our Lady of Willesden was not forgotten, and hope never wavered that the shrine would one day be restored.

In the middle years of the ninteenth century, a cautious spirit of renewal was abroad in the wake of the 1829 Act of Catholic Emancipation.

In 1885 a Catholic mission was opened at Willesden, and plans to reinstate the shrine were under way. Our Lady's words were being acted upon, some three hundred years after her appearance to the unfortunate Dr Crewkerne. Oak from an ancient tree in the parish churchyard was used for the new statue of Our Lady of Willesden. The fine dark figure stands today in the Lady chapel of the magnificent Catholic church that was built in 1931.

I joined other pilgrims to Willesden on the patronal feast of the shrine, 15 August, the Feast of the Assumption, and after Mass, Father Nicholas Schofield gave a talk on the history of the shrine. I had first seen the church on a dull January day, but now the sun flooded through the stained-glass windows of the shrine chapel and on to the walls painted by the Maltese artist, Carmel Cauchi. On the back wall there is a painting of the Annunciation, and behind the altar angels swirl around the skies surrounding the dark wooden statue of Our Lady of Willesden.

We walked back through the busy streets to the Willesden Junction Hotel. This once-imposing building, the familiar adjunct to all great railway stations, marked the rise in prosperity of Willesden when the huge junction was built in 1866. With its solid brick façade the hotel fell out of favour with travellers, but it has moved with the times by serving delicious Thai food.

We travelled the short distance by bus to the site of the original shrine in the Anglican church of St Mary of Willesden. Walking across the small Common and through an ancient lych gate, one had for the first time the sense of being in the country. We were surrounded by oak trees and leaning gravestones, their legends long since lost to lichen and the ravages of time.

Extraordinary events have taken place at St Mary's, and we discovered the miracle of the second Black Madonna. Weary of paying the annual fine of £13 for 'housing an idolatrous image', the vicar of St Mary's may have felt that he might as well be hanged for a sheep as for a lamb, and could see no reason against once again installing a statue of the Virgin in the church. The *History of the Church of St Mary* (ed. Cliff Wadsworth for the Willesden Local History Society) records that in 1911 'the Virgin returned to Willesden'. A fine statue was installed, but it was eventually felt that it did not do justice to the pre-Reformation original. In 1972 a new figure was carved out of lime wood by the sculptor Catharni Stern: a majestic Black Madonna with her Child, both with outstretched arms. The statue was dedicated by the Bishop of Willesden and placed in the newly-designated shrine chapel.

As if in response to this renewal of devotion, the ancient well was rediscovered in the cellar beneath the church in 1997. Holy water from the well is now available to the many pilgrims who come to visit Our Lady, and miracles are reported to have taken place.

On one occasion a parishioner who visited the shrine daily turned to Our Lady when her husband was seriously ill in hospital. The vicar visited the patient one evening, only to be sent back to collect water from the well which he had intended to bring but had forgotten. The man was understood to be dying, and the vicar remained through the night in prayer at the bedside with the family. In the morning the patient was still alive although mortally ill. The vicar left the hospital briefly. On his return he found the 'dying man' sitting up in bed eating a hearty breakfast.

On another occasion, water from the well was brought daily to a terminally-ill parishioner. After a few weeks, the woman was seen striding across the road towards the church. When this was remarked upon, she replied that she was coming to visit the Lord who had so graciously visited her on each day of her illness.

During a recent procession from the church of St Mary the decision was taken to walk through an area of known violence, and the passing of the statue of Our Lady was acknowledged with honour and respect. People came from their shops and places of work to watch her pass by.

Every year, two processions take place from the Catholic church of Our Lady of Willesden. In May 2002 the Cardinal Archbishop of Westminster, Cormac Murphy O'Connor, took part in the procession as it wound through the streets to the Convent of Jesus and Mary, where Benediction was held in the grounds. The October procession takes place through the streets of Willesden by torchlight.

In 1980 an ecumenical procession took place with participants from the Catholic church of Our Lady of Willesden and from the Anglican church of St Mary. This was an historic occasion, and it is to be hoped that it will be repeated. In the words of a booklet published to mark the occasion: 'Now Willesden once again has two Statues, the old oaken one and the lime wood one, both dark, both showing a loving and much loved Mother. Though separate, the Shrines show the same love – to Jesus Christ and his Mother. And maybe they will help separate Christians to understand and love one another more fully'.

As we left the Anglican church of St Mary, so remarkably restored, with its fine Lady chapel glowing in the candlelight, a violent thunderstorm raged around the churchyard. The sky was split by forked lightning and deafening thunder crashed around us. It was as if the feuds and rages of past centuries were venting their fury in childish tantrums. The candles before the Black Virgin merely flickered imperceptibly before resuming their gentle, strong light.

Shrine – Willesden

LOCATION/ DIRECTIONS	FROM M25 Exit J15, M4 towards London North Circular A406 Exit at Neasden A4058 Turn right into Neasden Lane (signposted Neasden Station) (St Mary's at end of the road) turn right at roundabout into Church Road Follow road round to Craven Park Road (about 1 mile) High Street, Harlesden (one way system) Turn right into Acton Lane (signposted County Court) Turn 1st right into Nicoll Road LONDON UNDERGROUND Bakerloo line Willesden Junction and Harlesden Stations (10 minute walk) BUSES 260 and 266
CONTACT TEL. NUMBERS	Our Lady of Willesden, The Presbytery, Nicoll Road Willesden London NW10 9AX Tel. 020 8965 4935
EMAIL ADDRESS	under construction
WEB SITE	under construction
TIMES OF SERVICES	Sunday (Saturday 6pm) 9.00am, 11.00am, and 5.30pm Weekdays 10.00am and 7.00pm Confessions, Sat. 10.30–11.30 and 5.00–5.45 Daily Exposition of Blessed Sacrament Monday to Saturday 10.30am and 6.30pm Sunday 3.30pm and 5.15pm

SPECIAL DATES/ EVENTS/ FESTIVALS/ PILGRIMAGES	2nd Sunday in May
	2nd Sunday in October: Torchlight Procession of Our Lady of Willesden
	Guild – President Cardinal Cormac Murphy O'Connor; Master of Guild – Mr. John Rick Miller
ROSARY GROUP	Every Monday to Saturday after Mass
	Guild of Our Lady, every Tuesday at 7.30pm
ANGLICAN CHURCH AND CONTACT TEL. NUMBERS	St Mary's (founded 938AD) 18 Neasden Lane London NW10 Tel. 020 8459 2167
	Shrine Prayers, 6.00pm Saturday Pilgrimage around Willesden on a Saturday in July after Mass
LOCAL ATTRACTIONS	The Grange Museum, (local history) Neasden Roundabout The Black Virgin of Willesden, The Shrine of Our Lady at St Mary's. Neasden Temple: Largest Hindu Temple outside India
GOOD PUBS	Thai Restaurant at Station Hotel, Willesden The Outside Inn, Neasden Shopping Centre
PLACES FOR PILGRIMS TO STAY	No specific!

28

Wintershall

WINTERSHALL

The story of Wintershall is the story of the journey in faith of one family, and although it is therefore their own, for many who come into contact with this phenomenon it is an inspiration. There is an almost tangible holiness here and at the same time, much happiness and laughter.

Leaving the busy A218 from Guildford the lane to Wintershall plunges down to the right, through a canopy of beech trees, past cottages surrounded by woodland and wild flowers, and eventually a blue sign appears, half hidden in the leaves, announcing 'St Francis Chapel'. Beyond the sign, gates open wide on to a long drive which lies between an avenue of chestnut trees.

This arrival is an invitation to a greater reality, for here at Wintershall there is a unique shrine of the Blessed Virgin. There is no specific shrine statue, although a beautiful figure of the Madonna and Child, carved by Sheila Mitchell, stands in front of the house. Rather, it is the estate, the fields and lakes, the rhododendron way which forms part of the Rosary Walk and the Stations of the Cross which are all under the patronage of Our Lady Queen of Peace, and are directed towards the greater glory of God.

The story begins many years ago when Peter and Ann Hutley and their family made several visits to the village of Medjugorje in the mountains of Bosnia, where six young people claim to have received visions of the Blessed Virgin since 1981. When war broke out in former Yugoslavia in 1991 the area around Medjugorje was regarded by many as an oasis of peace in a war-torn land. It has become a place of universal pilgrimage and prayer.

After one of their visits to Medjugorje in the 1980s the Hutleys returned with an unshakeable conviction that a 'monument' was to be made at Wintershall. How it should be made, or what it was to be, was far from clear – but a monument there was to be.

After much thought and consultation with friends and family, the decision was taken that part of the estate should be set aside for the creation of Stations of the Cross depicting the last journey of Christ from his condemnation by Pontius Pilate to his entombment. There is a place on the property that is reminiscent of a hill in Medjugorje, and although the one at Wintershall was almost impenetrable after the hurricane of 1987, with tangled limbs of fallen trees blocking the path, it nevertheless seemed an obvious choice for the Stations of the Cross. The project, named 'Operation Mustard Seed', involved not merely the creation of fourteen carved images of the Stations, but also the acquisition of land that did not at that time belong to the family but was acquired later. The land surrounded a large farm building that was known as 'Holly Barn'.

Notable sculptors were approached and were invited to submit ideas for the proposed figures to be used in the Stations. None responded and for a time the plan faltered. At the suggestion of a friend, Ann Hutley renewed her search for a sculptor in a different direction. Local art colleges and schools were approached, and the response was instant and enthusiastic.

At this stage the Hutleys were still unfamiliar with the custom of praying and meditating on the final journey of Christ at each of the fourteen Stations. A series of profoundly moving and thought-provoking images was nevertheless designed and produced by fourteen young artists, in prayerful consultation with the family, and after a great deal of scrambling up and down the steep and over-grown lane where it was proposed to place the Stations.

The depth of thought that occupied those involved is now obvious. The siting of each Station seems to have been chosen to concentrate the mind on each stage of the final journey of Jesus. At the fourteenth and final Station, the holy sepulchre is placed between the twisting roots of a tree that grows deep into the bank.

In May 1991 the dedication and blessing of the Stations took place in the warm spring sunshine. A small group followed the Anglican and Catholic clergy who led the group from one Station to the next, while children skipped along in the slipstream. This is now a regular event.

The creation of the Stations was well under way before Holly Barn and its surrounding fields finally became part of the estate. Situated at the summit of the hill, the barn is a traditional farm building with cattle stalls and mangers, and thoughts turned instinc-tively to the stable at Bethlehem.

The idea of a play came to mind almost immediately, and with the help of friends a Nativity play was prepared and performed. In the first year, the action of the play took place within the barn, the audience seated on bales of straw, as the story of the birth of Christ unfolded before them.

Now, more than ten years later, electricity and water are avail-able in Holly Barn. Sebastian Forbes, Professor of Music at Guildford University, is the musical director with his wife Tessa and the productions take place under the guidance of Ashley Herman. Friends taking part in the play endure the long trek up the wet and windy hill to Holly Barn for rehearsals, and the play is performed on several consecutive days. The audience grows every year as more and more people willingly turn out in all weathers, impervious to rain or snow.

The play begins outside the barn and overlooking the fields. The talking fades, and the audience becomes aware of small figures appearing in the distance out of the darkness. Joseph leads the donkey on which Mary is seated, and they move slowly across the fields towards the barn. The Angel Gabriel appears from the heights nearby, the shepherds with their sheep huddle around fires in the field, and we are transported to the Holy Land of two thou-sand years ago. We then turn from the field and walk into the barn with Mary and Joseph for the birth of Jesus. Angels sing and, with luck, the baby cries only briefly. Later on, the clattering of hooves announces the arrival of Herod's soldiers. For many people, this play has brought alive the true message of Christmas.

The Nativity Plays were the forerunner of a more ambitious plan. In 1993 a Passion play was performed which had been written by Peter Hutley, based on the Gospel stories of Christ's suffering and death. After the fourth year, the author announced the most ambitious plan of all. He intended to write an extended play, to cover the entire life of Christ from the Annunciation to the Ascension, which was to be performed during the year of the millennium.

The Life of Christ has been performed each year since the millennium and it is a life-changing experience for many of the thousands of people who descend on Wintershall at the end of June. They come from all over the world, many travelling vast distances to be present at England's Oberammergau.

Before the play begins, the audience settle themselves on rugs and chairs which have been carried across the grass, while members of the cast mingle with the crowd. The action begins with the Annunciation, as the words of the Angel Gabriel to Mary announce the miracle that is to be portrayed throughout the day, and we are enveloped in their world. As the play unfolds, the crowd walks from one scene to the next, accompanying the disciples and the followers of Jesus. Together, we become a single entity culminating in the joyful procession of Palm Sunday. The drama sweeps us along; the joy of the Baptism of Jesus and the miracles, the healing of the sick and the raising of Lazarus; Zacchaeus is revealed hiding in his tree among the audience. The mood changes as the drama of the trial and condemnation of Jesus unfold in all their brutality. The scene of the Crucifixion takes place on a distant hill and is witnessed in silence.

There is a slow and reflective walk to the place of the Resurrection and finally to the lake. Here the Apostles, at the Lord's word, cast their nets into the water, and Peter, in his joy, jumps from the boat to greet the risen Jesus. Then the final meal and Christ moves away towards his Ascension.

By now it is late afternoon, the shadows are lengthening and people reluctantly move away. It has been an unforgettable experience.

Although there is no specific shrine to Our Lady here, the title 'Our Lady of Wintershall' has been approved by the Bishop of Arundel and Brighton. On summer days of pilgrimage the statue of Mary is carried through the Rosary Way and up the lane past the Stations of the Cross to Holly Barn where Mass in celebrated. Afterwards an enormous cake is produced – for Our Lady's birthday on 8 September or for the particular feast day – and there is always enough for everyone, and tea as well.

Throughout the year, there are lectures and prayer days at Wintershall. Frequent visits are made to Medjugorje, often with groups of friends, and this provides the spiritual strength which is the source of all that happens here.

Standing beside the great Cross in front of Holly Barn, surveying the land as it falls away to fields and woodland as far as the eye can see, one feels that this is a place apart. The Wintershall estate has become a modern rendering of the medieval image of the mantle of the Blessed Virgin. Under her protection, people come in increasing numbers to pray, to make the Stations of the Cross, to take part in the Rosary Walks and to see the Nativity plays and the Life of Christ.

This is a remarkable and blessed place shared so generously by Peter and Ann Hutley with the thousands of people who come here. It is a place of joy untrammelled by the tragedies of history. At the start of the third millennium, it is a profound ecumenical statement that England is indeed the Dowry of Mary.

Shrine –Wintershall

LOCATION/ DIRECTIONS	From M25, exit J10 A3 Guildford A281 towards Horsham 3 miles from Bramley, turn right by bus shelter/sign post Turn right into Wintershall VISITS TO THE ESTATE ARE BY ARRANGEMENT ONLY
CONTACT TEL. NUMBERS	Wintershall Estate Bramley Nr Guildford Surrey Tel. 01483 892167
EMAIL ADDRESS	enquiries@wintershall-estate.com
WEB SITE	www.wintershall-estate.com
TIMES OF SERVICES	There are no regular services at the chapel but programmes of events are available from the estate office above.

Select Bibliography

Alton, D., *Pilgrim Ways – Catholic Pilgrimage Sites in Britain and Ireland*, St Paul's UK, 2001.

Azadi, Z., *Shrines to Our Lady Around the World*, Farrer Strauss and Young, New York, 1954.

Barlow, F., *Edward the Confessor*, Yale University Press, 1970.

Bridgett, Fr, *Our Lady's Dowry*, Burns & Oates, 1894.

British Publishing Company Ltd., *Coventry Under Fire – The Vicar of Holy Trinity Coventry*, Gloucester.

Bulter, A., *Butler's Lives of the Saints*, Virtue & Co. Ltd., 1954.

Carmelite Friars of Aylesford, *Image of Carmel – The Art of Aylesford*.

Catholic Encyclopedia on CD ROM.

Clare Priory, The Lavenham Press Ltd.

Clifton, M., and Goddard, D., *The Catholic Shrine of Our Lady of Consolation and St Francis – West Grinstead*, published by the Shrine of Our Lady of Consolation, West Grinstead.

Cross, F. L. and Livingstone, E. A., *The Oxford Dictionary of the Christian Church*, Oxford University Press.

Dalrymple, W., *From the Holy Mountain*, Flamingo.

Duffy, E., *The Stripping of the Altars*, Yale University Press, 1992.

Encyclical Letter of John Paul II, *Redemptoris Mater*.

Fraser, A., *King Charles II*, Wiedenfeld & Nicolson.

Fuller, R. C., *Warwick Street Church – A Short History and Guide*, 1973.

Gillett, M., *Shrines of Our Lady in England and Wales*, Samuel Walker Ltd., 1957.

—— *Famous Shrines of Our Lady*, vols I and II, Samuel Walker Ltd., 1952.

Gwyn. P., *The King's Cardinal – The Rise and Fall of Thomas Wolsey*, Pimlico, 1990.

Hackett, M. B., OSA, *The Austin Friars*, Augustinian Press, 1998.

Jones, M. K., and Underwood, M. G., *The King's Mother – Lady Margaret Beaufort, Countess of Richmond and Derby*, Cambridge University Press, 1992.

Knowles, D., *Monastic Order in England*, Cambridge University Press, 1940.

McGreal, W., O Carm, *The History of the Friars of Aylesford*, Jarrold Publishing.

Manley Hopkins, G., *Selected Poems*, Bloomsbury Poetry Classics, 1992.

Marsh, D., (Verger of Westminster Abbey), *The Story of Our Lady of Pew at Westminster*, 1975.

Obbard, E. R., CS, *The Land of Carmel*, Gracewing, 1999.

—— *A Year With Mary*, Canterbury Press, 1998.

Ollard, R., *This War Without an Enemy*, Hodder & Stoughton, 1976.

—— *The Escape of Charles II*, Robinson London, 1966.

Our Lady of Willesden, an account of the medieval shrine based on much new evidence, to mark the 450th anniversary of its demise in AD 1538, privately printed in 1988.

Pollard, M. and Godber, F., *The Guild of Our Lady of the Portal*, Dyllansow Truran, 1985.

Roden, F., *Coventry - Echoes of the Past*, Coventry Arts & Crafts Umbrella Organisation.

Rollings, P., *Walsingham - England's Nazareth*, RC National Shrine, Walsingham.

Roper, W., *The Life of St Thomas More*, Templegate.

Scholfield, N., *Our Lady of Willesden*, Genprint (Ireland) Ltd., 2001.

Smith, S., *The Madonna of Ipswich*, East Anglian Magazine Ltd., Ipswich, Suffolk, 1980.

Spencer Northcote DD, J., *Celebrated Sanctuaries of the Madonna*, Longmans Green and Co., 1868.

Storey, A., *Mount Grace Lady Chapel*, Highgate Publications (Beverley) Ltd., 2001.

Waterton, E., *Pietas Mariana Britannica*, St Joseph's Catholic Library, 1879.

Watkin, A., OSB, *The Story of Glastonbury*, Catholic Truth Society.

Index

Note: Page references in italics indicate line drawings. Names of major shrines are emboldened.